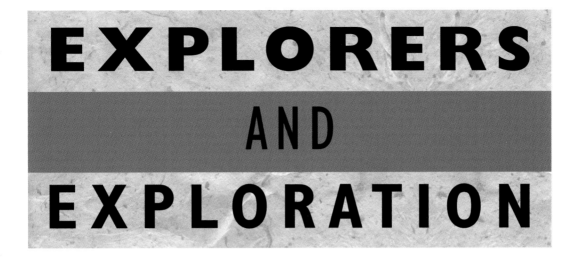

EXPLORERS
AND
EXPLORATION

NATURAL SCIENCES – POLAR EXPLORATION

Marshall Cavendish

New York • London • Singapore

Marshall Cavendish
99 White Plains Road
Tarrytown, New York 10591-9001

www.marshallcavendish.com

Consultants: Ralph Ehrenberg, former chief, Geography
and Map Division, Library of Congress, Washington, DC;
Conrad Heidenreich, former historical geography
professor, York University, Toronto; Shane Winser,
information officer, Royal Geographical Society, London

Contributing authors: Dale Anderson, Kay Barnham,
Peter Chrisp, Richard Dargie, Paul Dowswell, Elizabeth
Gogerly, Steven Maddocks, John Malam, Stewart Ross,
Shane Winser

MARSHALL CAVENDISH
Editor: Thomas McCarthy
Editorial Director: Paul Bernabeo
Production Manager: Michael Esposito

WHITE-THOMSON PUBLISHING
Editors: Alex Woolf and Steven Maddocks
Design: Ross George and Derek Lee
Cartographer: Peter Bull Design
Picture Research: Glass Onion Pictures
Indexer: Fiona Barr

ISBN 0-7614-7535-4 (set)
ISBN 0-7614-7542-7 (vol. 7)

Printed in China

08 07 06 05 04 5 4 3 2 1

color key	time period
▬▬▬▬▬	to 500
▬▬▬▬▬	500–1400
▬▬▬▬▬	1400–1850
▬▬▬▬▬	1850–1945
▬▬▬▬▬	1945–2000
▬▬▬▬▬	general articles

Library of Congress Cataloging-in-Publication Data
Explorers and exploration.
    p. cm.
  Includes bibliographical references (p.) and index.
  ISBN 0-7614-7535-4 (set : alk. paper) -- ISBN 0-7614-
7536-2 (v. 1) -- ISBN 0-7614-7537-0 (v. 2) -- ISBN 0-7614-
7538-9 (v. 3) -- ISBN 0-7614-7539-7 (v. 4) -- ISBN 0-7614-
7540-0 (v. 5) -- ISBN 0-7614-7541-9 (v. 6) -- ISBN 0-7614-
7542-7 (v. 7) -- ISBN 0-7614-7543-5 (v. 8) -- ISBN 0-7614-
7544-3 (v. 9) -- ISBN 0-7614-7545-1 (v. 10) -- ISBN 0-
7614-7546-X (v. 11)
  1. Explorers--Encyclopedias. 2. Discoveries in
geography--Encyclopedias. I. Marshall Cavendish
Corporation. II. Title.
  G80.E95 2005
  910'.92'2--dc22

                    2004048292

ILLUSTRATION CREDITS

AKG London: 484 (Erich Lessing), 486 (Gilles
Mermet), 489 (Bibliothèque Nationale, Paris), 498
(Kunstgewerbemuseum, Berlin), 499, 500 (Bibliothèque
Nationale, Paris), 503 (Erich Lessing), 504, 505, 507, 508,
510 (Erich Lessing), 511, 513, 514, 520, 524 (British
Library), 526 (Gold Museum, Bogotá, Colombia), 532,
535, 536, 537, 538, 539, 541 (Deutsches Museum,
Munich), 549, 551 (Museo Naval, Madrid), 552 (British
Library), 553, 554, 558.

Bridgeman Art Library: 485 (The Stapleton
Collection), 487 (Natural History Museum, London), 490
(Bibliothèque Nationale, Paris), 492 (National Maritime
Museum, London), 493, 494, 495 (Royal Geographical
Society, London), 497 (Bibliothèque Nationale, Paris),
501, 506 (Royal Geographical Society, London), 515,
517, 518, 527, 528 (Roger Perrin), 530, 540, 542, 543 (The
Stapleton Collection), 545, 547, 548, 556 (Royal
Geographical Society, London), 557 (Ken Welsh).

Peter Newark's American Pictures: 502, 522, 529, 533,
544, 550.

Science Photo Library, London: 488 (Dr. Ken
MacDonald), 496.

Cover: Martin Behaim's globe, 1492 (Bridgeman Art
Library / Lauros / Giraudon / Bibliothèque Nationale,
Paris).

CONTENTS

NATURAL SCIENCES

THE SURGE IN EXPLORATION that followed the European discovery of the Americas in the fifteenth century began a new chapter in world history. The Age of Exploration, as it became known, coincided with Europe's so-called scientific revolution. New interest in the natural sciences, such as geography, botany, and zoology, was stimulated by the wealth of new data gathered from natural environments all over the world. The result of this confluence of events was an entirely new way of understanding the world.

Below **In his *Revolutions of the Heavenly Spheres* (1543), Nicolaus Copernicus, the subject of this portrait, rejected Ptolemy's notion that a fixed earth was at the center of the universe.**

NON PAREM PAVLO GRATIÃ · REQVIRO
VENIAM PETRI NEQ, POSCO, SED QVAM
IN CRVCIS LIGNO DEDERAS LATRONI
SEDVLVS ORO

EXPLORING THE WORLD

The people of medieval Europe believed that there was nothing beyond the known world but chaos. A few scholars had read the translated works of ancient Greek philosophers, such as Ptolemy and Aristotle, which offered a more complete description of the earth (and of its place in the universe), but it was only when the first European explorers set off into the unknown—Portuguese sailors in the late fifteenth century were soon followed by Spanish, British, and Dutch—that it was possible to test some of the ancient theories.

The maritime explorers on these long ocean voyages of discovery found their way by using the stars to navigate (as sailors had done since ancient times). Given the importance of astronomy to navigation, it is unsurprising that the scientific revolution began with astronomy.

In medieval Europe, the Ptolemaic view of the universe remained largely unchallenged. The earth was thought to be stationary, with the sun and the stars moving in the sky above. In 1543 the Polish mathematician and astronomer Nicolaus Copernicus theorized that the earth was just one of several planets that revolve around the sun, the true center of the universe. New technologies, such as Galileo's telescopes, enabled people to observe the sky in more detail than ever

Francis Bacon 1561–1626

Until the sixteenth century, there was no separation of science and religion: understanding of the physical world was thoroughly infused with understanding of the nonphysical world. The influential English philosopher Francis Bacon encouraged people to make a distinction between knowledge of the natural world, which he called natural philosophy, and religion. *Novum Organum* (1620) presented a new scientific method for understanding the natural world. Bacon's method was based on direct observation, careful experimentation, and mathematical reasoning. In a sense modern science owes its birth to Bacon, who believed that scientific knowledge would give people more control over their life and prevent them from being powerless in the face of nature.

before. In 1627 Johannes Kepler published the first modern astronomical tables and proved that the planets move around the sun.

These concepts were radical at the time, as they contradicted the traditional religious teachings of the Christian Church and overturned people's notion of their place in the universe. The English philosopher and writer Francis Bacon (1561–1626) argued that new scientific theories need not be deemed to contradict religious faith, as scientific knowl-edge should be considered entirely separately from religion.

NEW NAMES FOR NEW DISCOVERIES

During the sixteenth century a revival in the study of natural history was led by physicians, who produced books of plant remedies known as herbals and examined the bodies of animals to learn about anatomy. Physicians began to expand their research to include plants and animals brought back by explorers.

Above **Francis Bacon advocated inductive reasoning, for which scientific data are of paramount importance. He intended to replace Aristotle's deductive reasoning, which was based on logic and argument.**

BOTANY

The science of botany (the study of plants) is closely associated with exploration. Perhaps the greatest botanist was the Swede Carolus Linnaeus (Carl von Linné). Linnaeus's specimens were brought from all over the world by his students, one of whom, Philibert de Commerson, joined the circumnavigation of Louis-Antoine de Bougainville (1766–1769)—the first French voyage to include scientists.

Linnaeus's most famous protegés were the English scientist Joseph Banks (1743–1820) and the Swede Daniel Solander (d. 1782), who both sailed aboard the *Endeavour* on James Cook's first Pacific voyage (1768–1771). Their findings included the kangaroo and perhaps as many as one thousand previously unknown species. When Banks later became president of the Royal Society, he requested that a scientist travel with every British expedition. England soon accumulated natural history collections from all around the world.

With Cook on his second voyage across the Pacific (1772–1775) were the father and son naturalists Johann Reinhold Forster (1729–1798) and Johann Georg Adam Forster (1754–1794). Their findings inspired another German scientist and explorer, Alexander von

Right **Philibert de Commerson found this plant in the vicinity of Rio de Janeiro in 1767 and named it** *Boungainvillea spectabilis,* **after the leader of the expedition.**

1543
By suggesting that the earth moves around the sun, Nicolaus Copernicus overturns the popularly held view of the universe

1620
In his *Novum Organum,* Francis Bacon proposes a new scientific method based on data and observation.

1753–1758
Carolus Linnaeus publishes his system of classifying plants and animals by genus and species.

1768–1771
Joseph Banks and Daniel Solander sail with Captain James Cook to Australia.

1799–1804
Alexander von Humboldt and Aimé Bonpland gather a vast amount of scientific data in South America.

1831–1836
Charles Darwin sails with Robert Fitzroy aboard the *Beagle.*

1853
First public aquarium is founded in London.

1854–1862
Alfred Russel Wallace travels through the Malay Archipelago.

1990s
Marine biologists study the unique ecosystems surrounding hydrothermal vents far beneath the surface of the ocean.

Botanical Nomenclature

*T*o discuss and share their discoveries with one another, European scientists needed a system of names (a nomenclature), in a common language, to describe the plants and animals being brought back by explorers. The solution was provided by the Swedish botanist Carolus Linnaeus (1707–1778). Between 1753 and 1758 Linnaeus published (in Latin) a system of classification for plants and animals, based on class, order, genus, and species, that is still in use. Apart from one journey to Lapland, an Arctic region of Scandinavia, Linneaus chose not to travel himself. Instead, he encouraged his students to collect plants for him from around the world.

Below **The system of naming plants developed by Carolus Linnaeus is still used by botanists.**

Humboldt. From 1799 to 1804 Humboldt and his companion, Aimé Bonpland, mapped, measured, and sketched as much as possible of the South American geography, climate, people, and wildlife. Humboldt's account of his journey, *Personal Narrative,* in turn convinced the English scientist Charles Darwin (1809–1882) to take part in a voyage of exploration. Darwin joined Captain Robert Fitzroy's *Beagle* voyage, from 1831 to 1836.

SURVIVAL OF THE FITTEST

When Darwin set off, most people in the Christian world still believed the biblical story of the world's creation. On the Galápagos Islands, Darwin found that sailors could tell which island they were on by looking at the birds. He wondered if these birds had evolved from a common ancestor (rather than having been created by God), but it was many years before he would admit in public to such blasphemous ideas.

Darwin was not alone. Alfred Russel Wallace (1823–1913) and his friend Henry Walter Bates (1825–1892), both amateur naturalists, set off for the Amazon in 1848. Bates collected butterflies and observed that many of them were able to mimic other creatures to avoid being eaten. Wallace spent four years in the Amazon and then eight in Southeast Asia, where, on a journey of some fourteen thousand miles (22,500 km), he collected around 127,000 plants and animals.

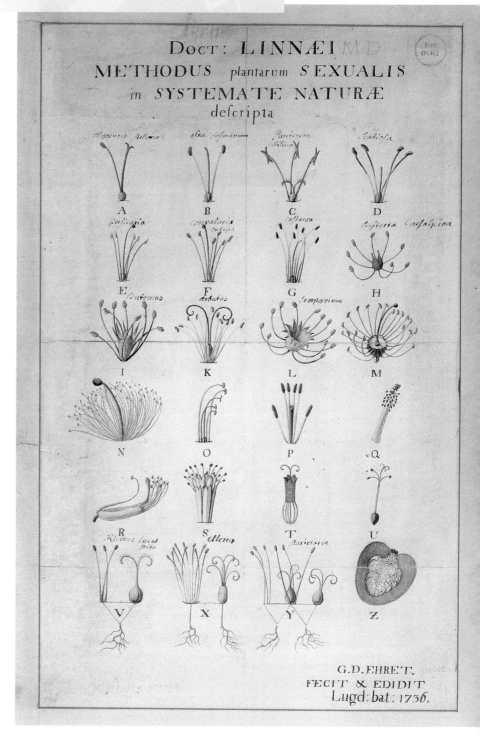

Right **These giant tube worms were photographed on an underwater pillar of cooled lava on the northern East Pacific Rise, part of the volcanically active mid-ocean ridge system, at a depth of 8,530 feet (2,600 m), where it was previously thought no life-form could exist.**

This comment was made by the naturalist Thomas Henry Huxley (1825–1895) when he read Darwin's *Origin of Species*:

How extremely stupid not to have thought of that.

While in South America, Wallace read a book that had also influenced Darwin. Robert Malthus's *Essay on the Principle of Population* (1798) suggested that if population increases were not kept in check by natural forces, a struggle for survival would result. Both Wallace and Darwin concluded that such struggles happen continually in the natural world and that in nature only the fittest survive. When Darwin's *Origin of Species* was published in 1859, Wallace was happy to have Darwin take the credit (and face the public outcry).

MARINE BIOLOGY

Several new branches of natural sciences emerged during the nineteenth and twentieth centuries. Philip Henry Gosse (1810–1888), for instance, worked in the field of marine biology and, in 1853, helped found the world's

first public aquarium in London's Regent's Park. During the last years of the twentieth century, marine biologists found previously unknown life-forms living 8,000 feet (2,440 m) beneath the ocean in the hot, mineral-rich waters gushing from hydrothermal vents (cracks along ridges on the ocean floor).

More than five hundred years after Columbus reached the New World, new discoveries are still regularly being made in the natural sciences. Scientists remain unclear about how many species there are on the planet. Estimates range from five to ten million—a figure that does not include bacteria and viruses. As many remain unclassified, there is plenty of work for naturalists to do.

SEE ALSO

- Astronomy • Banks, Joseph
- Bougainville, Louis-Antoine de • Cook, James
- Darwin, Charles • Fitzroy, Robert • Geography
- Humboldt, Alexander von • Scandinavia
- Wallace, Alfred Russel

NAVIGATION

THE WORD *NAVIGATION* DERIVES FROM THE LATIN *navis,* meaning "ship," and *agere,* "to drive," and describes the science of directing the course of a ship at sea. The term may also describe any method used by an explorer to establish current position or to plot the route already taken and the route to come. Whether sailing the oceans, crossing deserts on foot, or flying in airplanes, all explorers were—and are—required to be navigators.

EARLY NAVIGATION

Long before any navigational instruments were invented, sailors were finding their way using the sun and the stars, a method known as celestial navigation. In its simplest form celestial navigation uses the sun's daily journey across the sky from east to west as a means of locating the four main compass points (north, south, east, and west). At night the ancient Greeks used the Great Bear group of stars, which dominates the northern sky, as a guide to direction. This constellation was of such importance that the Greek word for "bear," *arctos,* was also the word for "north." In the *Odyssey* (c. 750 BCE) Homer describes his hero, Odysseus, steering his ship eastward by keeping the Great Bear on his left.

Winds were equally important to early navigators. Around the world there is a recognizable pattern of prevailing (frequently occurring) winds. In the Indian Ocean, for example, the wind blows from the southwest from April until October and then reverses direction, blowing from the northeast from November until the end of March. Since ancient times seafarers have used these winds to guide them on trading voyages between Africa and India.

Below **In this sixteenth-century French picture, a navigator is taking a sighting on the Pole Star to discover where north lies. Using the compass rose, he can then locate all other directions.**

In the Mediterranean winds were given names, often those of the places they blew from. The Romans called the southwest wind Africus because it blew from Africa. Navigators often thought in terms of these winds rather than directions. Instead of sailing northeast, for example, Roman sailors would think of themselves as sailing "with Africus."

LOOKING FOR LAND

Just as there are landmarks on land, in the open sea there are seamarks, signs that may help a navigator find his way. For example, a type of white, puffy cloud called cumulus (from the Latin for "heap") is usually formed by moisture rising from land. An experienced sailor will spot cumulus clouds long before the land beneath comes into view. Other useful seamarks are floating twigs and weeds and changes in the color, temperature, and depth of the water, which may be tested by lowering a weighted line over the side.

Birds are also useful to navigators. For example, every spring vast flocks of geese fly from their winter feeding grounds in Ireland to summer breeding grounds in Iceland. Iceland was first discovered around 800 CE by Irish monks, who may well have set their course by following the geese.

Viking explorers developed an ingenious method of finding land. They would take captured land birds, such as ravens and doves, to sea and free one from time to time. A bird in the air can see much farther than a sailor on a ship. If the bird saw nothing on the horizon, it would return to the ship, but if it saw land, it would fly in that direction, and the sailors could follow.

Left **In this fifteenth-century illustration of ships crossing the Indian Ocean, the navigator on the left uses an astrolabe to observe the position of certain stars (and thus estimate his latitude).**

Floki Vilgerdarsen was the Viking explorer who, around the year 865, gave Iceland its name. According to a twelfth-century Icelandic story, he found the land by using ravens, birds sacred to the god Odin:

Floki had taken three ravens to sea with him. When he released the first, it flew back in the direction of the island they had come from. The second flew high into the air and then back to the ship. The third flew straight ahead in the direction in which they found land.

The Book of the Settlements

VIKING NAVIGATION

From the eighth to the eleventh centuries, on long voyages out into the North Sea and the North Atlantic, Viking explorers from Norway discovered and settled the Shetland, Orkney, and Faeroe island groups, as well as Iceland and Greenland and, probably, the continent of North America.

In order to make these voyages and return safely to Norway, the Vikings depended on the navigator's making accurate calculations of the ship's latitude (north-south position). By day the navigator used the height of the sun, which was lower in the sky the farther north one traveled. By night he used the Pole Star, so called because it appears in the sky almost directly above the North Pole. The farther south the Vikings sailed, the lower the Pole Star appeared to sink. A sailor could roughly judge the height of the sun and the Pole Star by noting how far up the ship's mast they appeared. Vikings are also thought to have measured the sun's height using simple wooden sundials, upright sticks that cast a shadow on the ground. The farther south they sailed, the higher in the sky the midday sun rose—and thus the shorter the shadow cast by the stick.

The Compass and the Chart

A compass is an instrument consisting of a floating magnetic needle that always points north (the earth itself is magnetic, and the needle points to the magnetic north pole). The compass was invented by the Chinese before 250 CE, but the earliest Chinese reference to a compass used at sea dates from much later, in the eleventh century. By the late twelfth century the compass was also in use in the Mediterranean, though it is not known whether it had come there from China or had been invented independently.

In the thirteenth century Italian mapmakers began to make charts of the Mediterranean Sea, showing compass directions as lines from port to port. These charts, which also showed estimated distances, were called portolans. Simply by placing a compass on a portolan, a navigator could work out the direction to sail in order to reach the destination port.

Together the compass and the chart made it possible to practice a new type of navigation, called dead reckoning. This method of navigation requires a sailor to keep track of the distance and direction sailed every day and to mark the ship's changing position on a chart.

To work out the distance traveled, a navigator needed to know his ship's speed over a set period of time. Time was marked by a sandglass, turned every half hour. In the fifteenth century a ship's speed was measured by watching bubbles or chips of wood float past. In the sixteenth century a rope with a wooden float at one end, tied with knots at regular intervals, was used. The float was dropped over the side, and the rope was paid out for half a minute. Then it was pulled in, and the knots were counted: the more knots, the faster the ship's speed. (One nautical mile per hour, the standard unit of speed at sea, is still known as a knot).

Above **From the fifteenth century, sandglasses, such as this one, marked time at sea. It took exactly half an hour for the sand to pour through the glass.**

Another Viking navigation method was latitude sailing. A Viking explorer knew how high the sun appeared at midday in his home port in Norway. Out on the ocean he would sail north or south until the sun was in the same position. He knew then that he was in the same latitude as his home port and that if he sailed due east he would reach home.

Left **This pivoting ship's compass, shielded from the elements by its wooden case, was made in 1720 in Saint Petersburg, Russia.**

Around 1205 the French poet Guyot de Provins wrote one of the first European accounts of the compass. At the time Europeans believed that the needle was attracted by the Pole Star:

By virtue of the magnet stone they practise an art which cannot lie. Taking this ugly dark stone, to which iron will attach itself of its own accord, they find the right point on it which they touch with a needle. Then they lay the needle in a straw and simply place it in water, where the straw makes it float. Its point then turns exactly to the star. There is never any doubt about it; it will never deceive. When the sea is dark and misty, so that neither star nor Moon can be seen, they put a light beside the needle, and then they know their way.

Quoted in E. G. R. Taylor, *The Haven-Finding Art*

New Instruments

A measurement of the vertical angle of the sun and stars above the horizon enabled a good navigator to calculate the latitude of his ship with reasonable accuracy. From the fifteenth century on, various navigational instruments became available to help navigators take such measurements. The earliest, the quadrant, evolved from the astrolabe, an ancient star-measuring device. The sixteenth, seventeenth, and eighteenth centuries saw the invention of more accurate instruments, including the marine astrolabe, the cross-staff, the back staff, the octant, and the sextant. Until the invention of the chronometer in the mid-eighteenth century, however, no similar instrument existed to help a ship's navigator calculate longitude (east-west position). The only method of working out longitude at sea was dead reckoning, a procedure that often gave inaccurate measurements.

Electronic Navigation

The twentieth century saw the invention of a number of electronic navigation instruments and systems. Among the new technologies was sonar (sound navigation and ranging). Sonar devices beam sound waves through a body of water. The time taken for the sound waves to return indicates the depth of the water or the presence of any major objects or geological features under the surface.

Above **This pocket sextant, which was made around 1831 and belonged to the English naturalist Charles Darwin, has a revolving arm with a magnifying glass, used to read the scale.**

c. 430 BCE
The Greek historian Herodotus describes the use of the lead and line to measure water depth.

c. 180 CE
The Greek geographer Ptolemy draws a map that includes lines of longitude and latitude.

c. 250
The magnetic compass is invented in China.

c. 865
Using ravens to help find land, the Viking explorer Floki Vilgerdarsen reaches Iceland.

c. 1180
The magnetic compass is in use in Europe.

c. 1280
The earliest known European sea chart, the Carte Pisane, is drawn up.

1450
Use of the quadrant at sea is reported for the first time.

1480s
Marine astrolabes are first used on voyages by the Portuguese.

1492–1493
Columbus uses dead reckoning to cross the Atlantic and return safely home.

c. 1594
John Davis invents the back staff.

Below **This English marine chronometer, made in 1792 by Josiah Emery, measures hours, minutes, and seconds on separate dials and is housed in a baize-lined wooden case.**

Radar (radio detection and ranging) technology is based on principles similar to those of sonar. A radar device emits radio waves (as opposed to sound waves) and, by analyzing the returning echoes, builds up a picture of the surrounding area, including the presence of any obstacles. A navigator at sea in foggy weather or during the hours of darkness can use radar to detect the presence of icebergs, other ships, or the coastline.

The Longitude Problem

For centuries mathematicians and scientists struggled with the problem of how to work out the longitude of a ship at sea. They knew that the answer was linked to time. For every fifteen degrees longitude traveled east or west, there is a time difference of one hour. If a navigator could compare local time at sea with the time at his home port, he would know from the difference how far east or west he had traveled.

In 1522 Gemma Frisius, a Flemish mathematician, argued that the answer to the problem lay in building a clock whose mechanism could cope—on a voyage lasting several months—with the movement of a ship, which could be violent, and with changes in temperature and humidity, which could be extreme.

The solution was provided in 1759 by an English clock maker named John Harrison. Harrison built a chronometer (literally, "time measurer") that did not lose time on long journeys. The chronometer was mass-produced in nineteenth century factories and became as important a navigational tool as the compass and the sextant.

1731
John Hadley devises the octant, an instrument in the shape of an eighth of a circle with a configuration of mirrors that allows the user to observe and calculate the position of heavenly bodies.

1757
John Campbell builds a sextant, an instrument in the shape of a sixth of a circle that gives more accurate readings than those of an octant.

1759
John Harrison builds a chronometer, an instrument that keeps accurate time at sea.

1918
Sonar technology is developed in the United States and Britain.

1919–1935
The Scottish scientist Sir Robert Alexander Watson-Watt developes radar.

1930s
The United States develops the shoran and loran navigation systems.

1994
GPS (Global Positioning System) comes into operation.

Right **On this ship's radar screen, the ship is located at the center, and the concentric green circles each represent a distance of one-quarter of a mile (402 m). As the ship's radar beam sweeps around, an image is built up of nearby objects that reflect the beam. This screen shows a coastline (left) and the harbor where the ship is docked (center).**

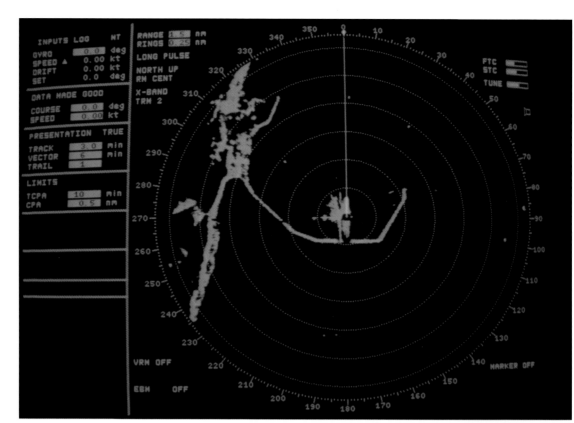

Shore-based radio transmitters are used in systems called loran (long-range navigation) and shoran (short-range navigation), first developed in the United States in the 1930s. Equipment on board a ship picks up radio signals transmitted from two different stations. A computer then uses the time difference between the two signals to work out the ship's precise position.

Lunar Distance Method

*D*uring the sixteenth century, astronomers and mathematicians published books of astronomical data called almanacs, which contained lists of the angle of the moon in relation to various stars when viewed at different times from a given longitude, such as Greenwich (0°). A navigator at sea made his own observations of the moon and looked through the almanac to find out the time in Greenwich when the moon appeared in precisely the same position. By comparing the two times he worked out his longitude. The lunar distance method involved complex calculations and depended on measurements of great accuracy. It became practical only with the invention of the sextant in the middle of the eighteenth century.

Since 1994 the Global Positioning System (GPS) has provided navigators with a simple, reliable, and instantaneous way of establishing their position. Twenty-four satellites in continual fixed orbit around the earth transmit radio signals giving their position and the time. A receiver picks up signals from three different satellites and calculates its own position. GPS receivers are small enough to be carried in a pocket or mounted on the dashboard of a car and may be used by amateur as well as professional navigators.

Although electronic equipment is a vital aid to navigation, no electronic technology is infallible. Professional navigators still learn the basic skills of dead reckoning and celestial observation for use in an emergency.

SEE ALSO
- Astronomical Instruments • Astronomy
- Chronometer • Dead Reckoning
- Global Positioning System
- Latitude and Longitude
- Navigational Instruments

NAVIGATIONAL INSTRUMENTS

THROUGHOUT HISTORY EXPLORERS traveling by air, land, and sea have depended on a number of navigational instruments—from the magnetic compass to the handheld GPS (Global Positioning System) receiver—to establish their position when there were no recognizable landmarks in the vicinity. An explorer may use positional information to plot the next stage of a route, to assess whether it is worth continuing in the same direction, or to record the exact location of a new discovery.

Below **The Italian explorer Amerigo Vespucci uses his astrolabe on a coast somewhere in the Americas—the continents that were named after him.**

LEAD AND LINE

The oldest known navigational instrument is the lead and line—a lead weight fixed to the end of a rope that was lowered over the side of a boat or ship to measure the depth of the water. This information was useful because the sea typically becomes shallower as it draws near to land.

The underside of the lead was greased with sticky tallow (animal fat) to bring up samples from the bed of a river or the sea. Seabed reveals much to an experienced navigator. In the fifth century BCE, for example, the Greek historian Herodotus was a passenger on a voyage to Egypt. According to Herodotus, the sailors knew that they were a day's sail from their destination when they dropped the lead over the side and brought up yellow mud—silt washed out to sea by Egypt's mighty Nile River.

THE COMPASS

The Chinese are thought to have invented the compass, which they called the point-south needle, sometime before 250 CE. At first they used the compass not for navigation but to plan buildings and tombs in such a way that the structures, when completed, would be in harmony with the invisible forces of energy that the Chinese believed ran through the natural world.

By the twelfth century, Chinese and European seafarers were using simple compasses as an aid to navigation. Early compasses were needles that had been magnetized (made magnetic) by being placed in contact with a lump of magnetite (magnetic iron ore). Hung from a thread or floated in a bowl of water, the needle would point north, toward the earth's magnetic pole. In the Mediterranean, by the 1300s the needle had been stuck to a circular piece of card, which was painted to show directions, and placed on a pivot in a box. This arrangement was much more suitable than a bowl of water for use on a ship. In the sixteenth century, the compass was mounted on double rings and housed in a wooden box called a binnacle. The binnacle kept the instrument level in spite of the rolling of the ship.

One problem with the compass is that the earth's magnetic north pole, to which the needle points, is not in the same place as the geographic North Pole. At the beginning of the twenty-first century, for example, magnetic north lay in the Canadian Arctic and was moving roughly northwest at a rate of around 26 miles (40 km) a year. Thus, from many places on the earth, a compass needle points not to true north but to the northwest or northeast. This phenomenon, known as compass variation, greatly troubled fifteenth- and sixteenth-century explorers. From the 1530s Portuguese navigators recorded the compass variations they found in different locations. This information, recorded in lists and shown as lines on maps, allowed navigators to apply the appropriate correction to their compass courses.

Above **This magnificent sixteenth-century German compass is decorated with images of the Roman gods after which the planets are named, Mars, Venus, Mercury, and others.**

This excerpt is taken from a twelfth-century account of Chinese navigation methods, which included the use of the lead and line and the compass ("point-south needle"):

The commanders of the vessels know the appearance of the coasts. By night they steer by the stars and by day by the sun. When the sun is hidden, they observe the point-south needle, or they use a line which is a hundred feet long and ends in a lump with which they get up mud from the bottom of the sea. From the smell which their mud gives off, they know where they are.

Tchou Yu

Quadrant and Astrolabe

From the fifteenth century, European seafarers used special instruments to measure the angle of the sun above the horizon at midday and of the Pole Star at night. The position of either celestial body could be used to work out a ship's latitude, that is, its north-south position. The first such instruments were the quadrant and the astrolabe. Invented in ancient times by Greek astronomers, they were not used by Europeans at sea until the fifteenth century.

In its simplest form, the quadrant is a quarter circle cut out of a sheet of metal or wood, with a weighted thread suspended from one corner. Along one of the straight edges are two sighting holes. A navigator looked through the sighting holes at the Pole Star. He then pinched the thread against a scale on the bottom edge, which gave the measurement of latitude. Quadrants were less useful for measuring the sun, for it was dangerous to look directly into the sun through a quadrant's sights.

The astrolabe consists of a heavy bronze disk hanging from a metal ring. Engraved on the main disk is a network of lines representing celestial coordinates. A solid outer band represents the zodiac, and a rotating inner disk (called a rete) represents the revolving stars. A straight arm, called an alidade, enabled the user to sight celestial objects in the sky.

Above **This gilded brass quadrant, considerably more elaborate than those used at sea, was constructed around 1618 by the leading German instrument maker Christoph Treschler.**

A Spanish traveler who made a long sea voyage in 1573 described in a letter the difficulty of using an astrolabe at sea:

You should see the pilot . . . taking up his astrolabe at midday, looking up at the sun and trying to make it shine through the holes on his instrument, and failing, and trying to adjust it. He finally pronounces judgement on the height of the sun; sometimes he has it 1,000 degrees too high, sometimes he is so far below it that it would take him 1,000 years to reach it. . . . They know that they never get it right. . . . The width of a pinhead on their instrument will put you 500 miles out in your reckoning.

Eugenio de Salazar

Quadrants and astrolabes were more accurate on land than on the rolling deck of a ship. They were especially useful on shore, where they enabled explorers to work out the latitude of newly discovered lands.

In 1488 the Portuguese explorer Bartolomeu Dias found the southernmost tip of Africa, which was later named the Cape of Good Hope. Dias used a maritime astrolabe to work out the cape's latitude and returned home not only with the exciting news of his discovery but also with an accurate map for future sailors to use.

CROSS-STAFF AND BACK STAFF

The cross-staff, which came into maritime use in the 1500s, was more accurate at sea than a quadrant or astrolabe. The navigator pointed a long pole at a point midway between the horizon and the celestial body whose height was to be measured. He then slid a cross-piece, set at right angles, until its ends lined up with the horizon and the sun or star.

Around 1594 the English navigator John Davis invented the back staff, so called because the user stood with his back to the sun. Aiming the instrument at the horizon, which he viewed through a slit in a metal plate at the far end of the staff, he slid a cross-piece until it cast a shadow onto the plate. The back staff was a big improvement over the cross-staff, for the user had to aim at only a single target—the horizon—and he did not

Above **This copper astrolabe was constructed by Ahmad ibn Khalaf in Iraq in the ninth century.**

have to look directly into the sun. The disadvantage of the back staff was that it could not be used at night to measure the height of the Pole Star.

OCTANT AND SEXTANT

In 1731 the English inventor John Hadley built an instrument called an octant (eighth), because it was in the form of an eighth of a circle. Attached to it were two mirrors, one of which was half silvered, so that the observer could look through it. The second mirror was attached to a movable arm. The observer looked at the horizon through the first mirror and then moved the arm until the second mirror reflected light from the sun or a star onto the first mirror. He could then read the angle of the sun or star from a scale. "With this instrument," wrote Hadley with justifiable pride, "though the ship rolls ever so much … the observer has the same advantage of making the observation as if he took it in smooth water, and the instrument was held still without motion."

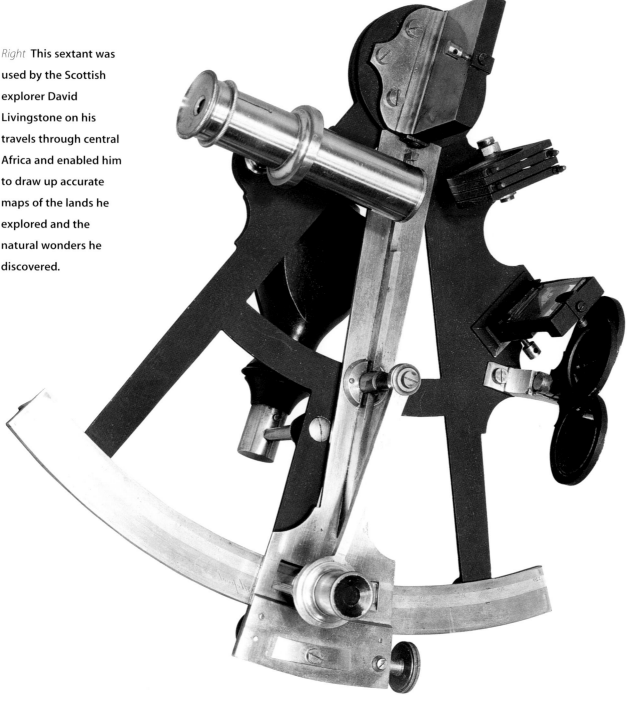

Right **This sextant was used by the Scottish explorer David Livingstone on his travels through central Africa and enabled him to draw up accurate maps of the lands he explored and the natural wonders he discovered.**

Gyrocompass

Since the nineteenth century, ships have been built with hulls containing iron, which interferes with the functioning of magnetic compasses. In 1908 an American inventor, Elmer Sperry, invented a compass mounted on a gyroscope, a spinning wheel constructed so that it is free to move in any direction. Sperry's gyrocompass moved in conjunction with the earth's spin and gravity and was able to indicate north without being affected by magnetism. As gyrocompasses are much more reliable than magnetic compasses, they are carried on board modern ships, submarines, planes, and spacecraft.

Left On December 12, 1911, the Norwegian explorer Roald Amundsen used his sextant to take a reading of the sun's position. The reading confirmed that he had reached the South Pole.

In 1757 another Englishman, Captain John Campbell, improved the octant by adding a telescopic sight and increasing its size to a sixth of a circle. This new instrument, called a sextant, could measure larger angles than an octant. It could also be fitted with a colored glass filter, to protect the user's eyes from the sun as he took measurements. The most accurate navigational instrument invented up to that time, the sextant was used by explorers from the late eighteenth century onward. In 1770 James Cook used a sextant on his Pacific voyage to work out his longitude by measuring the angles and distances between the moon and various stars. Polar explorers, including Robert Scott, Roald Amundsen, and Robert E. Peary, used sextants to locate the North and South Poles. Sextants were used in the African jungle, in the deserts of Australia, and by pilots on long airplane journeys.

SEE ALSO
- Chronometer
- Dead Reckoning
- Navigation

NETHERLANDS

THE DUTCH GOLDEN AGE STARTED after independence from Spain was won in 1579 and lasted for around a hundred years. The Netherlands' preeminence in the field of exploration was founded on its control of the spice trade and under-pinned by a powerful economy and by remarkable achievements in cartography and shipbuilding. From the late seventeenth century the rivalry among European nations, expressed in mercantilist economic policy as well as in warfare, put a great deal of pressure on the Netherlands. By the end of the eighteenth century, the Dutch fleet had suffered a marked decline.

TRANSPORT HUB

Three great rivers, the Rhine, the Maas, and the Schelde, empty into the sea along the coast of the Netherlands. By the end of the fifteenth century, Dutch ports were at the crossroads of European trade. During the early part of the sixteenth century, Spanish and Portuguese voyages uncovered the possibility of direct sea routes between Europe and Asia. Portugal began to see considerable profits from the trade in spices from the East Indies (present-day Indonesia). Toward the end of the century, the newly independent Netherlands began to look for a way into the spice trade.

IN SEARCH OF A NORTHEAST PASSAGE

The first Dutch voyages in search of a route to Asia were made to the northeast by Willem Barents (c. 1550–1597). Between 1594 and 1596 Barents piloted three Arctic voyages across the sea that came to bear his name. On the third Barents's ships were frozen in, and he was forced to winter in the Arctic. In June 1597 his party set sail for the mainland; Barents died within a week of setting out. Although Dutch attention turned to southern routes, Barents's charts of the Russian Arctic were of enormous value to later explorers searching for a northeast passage.

Left **This view of the bustling harbor of Amsterdam was painted in 1674 by the Dutch artist Ludolf Backhuysen.**

FIRST VOYAGES

From 1595 to 1597 Cornelis Houtman led the first Dutch voyage to the East Indies via southern Africa. In 1599 Jacob van Neck and Wijbrandt van Warwijck returned to the Netherlands with an extremely profitable cargo of cloves and nutmeg. Van Neck and Warwijck had taken a route directly from the Cape of Good Hope via the island of Mauritius to the Sunda Strait, the gateway to the East Indies—a route to the spices that bypassed the Portuguese settlements around the rim of the Indian Ocean.

THE DUTCH EAST INDIA COMPANY

In 1602 several Dutch merchant companies united to form the United East India Company (its Dutch name was *Vereenigde Oost-indische Compagnie*, or VOC). Granted a monopoly on all Dutch trade in the East Indies, the VOC set up several posts, the most important of which was at Bantam, at the northern end of the Sunda Strait.

Between 1614 and 1618 the VOC, under Jan Pieterszoon Coen (1587–1629), secured monopolies throughout the East Indies. In 1619 Coen established a new fortified headquarters at Batavia (present-day Jakarta). Over the next twenty-five years, Coen and his sucessors, Anthony van Diemen (1593–1645) and Joan Maetsuyker (1606–1678), built a network of fortified settlements throughout southern and eastern Asia and, in 1652, a resupply post at Cape Town.

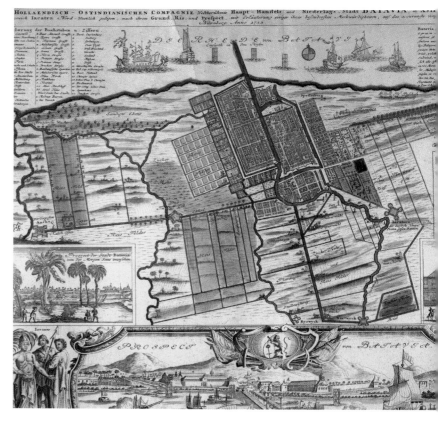

NEW HOLLAND

As the first European sighting of Australia was made by a Dutch explorer, Willem Jansz (in 1605), the country was known until the nineteenth century as New Holland. Under van Diemen the VOC sent Abel Tasman (c. 1603–c. 1659) on two voyages around New Holland in the 1640s. Tasman charted significant areas of the Australian coast, but the apparent lack of wealth discouraged the Dutch from any exploration of the Australian interior.

CAPE HORN

In 1615 Jakob Le Maire (c. 1585–1616) hired Willem Schouten (c. 1570–1625) to find a new

Above **This city plan of Batavia (the present-day Indonesian capital of Jakarta), engraved in 1733, incorporates depictions of local peoples and wildlife.**

The Roaring Forties

Until the seventeenth century the only charted routes across the Indian Ocean were the Arab trade routes (also used by the Portuguese) that hugged the coasts. Dutch sailors heading for Southeast Asia faced an extremely long voyage at the mercy of cyclones and unpredictable monsoon winds. In 1611 Hendrick Brouwer sailed far to the south of Cape Town and came upon constant westerly winds between forty and fifty degrees south latitude. This wind system, known as the Roaring Forties, enabled the Dutch to cut the typical length of a voyage to the East Indies from sixteen months to six months.

Below **Willem Schouten's account of his voyage around Cape Horn with Jakob Le Maire was published in 1619 and carried illustrations by the celebrated Flemish engraver Theodore de Bry.**

route around South America. The route then in use, through the Strait of Magellan, was dangerous and in the control of the VOC, whose restrictions Le Maire hoped to evade. The men passed the opening of the Strait of Magellan and in 1616 rounded the tip of South America, which Schouten named Cape Horn after Hoorn, his birthplace. Upon arrival in Java in the East Indies, Schouten and Le Maire were arrested by VOC officials.

Right **Abraham**
Ortelius's 1570
Theatrum Orbis
Terrarum (known in
English as *Epitome of*
the Theater of the
World) was the most
popular atlas of its
time and remained in
print continuously until
1612. During Ortelius's
lifetime the Antarctic
remained unexplored.
Thus, his greatest
error—his depiction of
a vast southern
continent—long went
undetected.

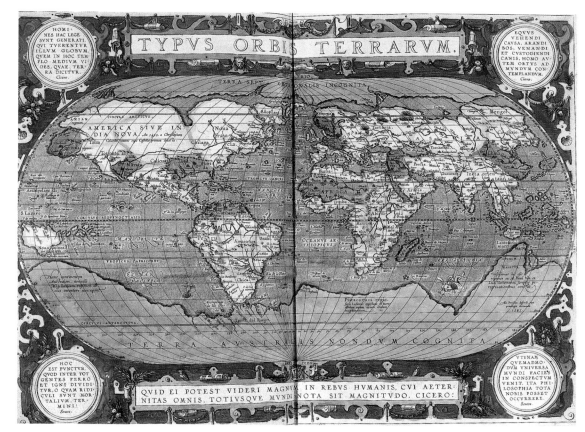

MAPMAKING IN THE NETHERLANDS

During the sixteenth and seventeenth centuries the Netherlands was one of the world's academic centers. The Dutch made significant contributions to the sciences that supported exploration, such as shipbuilding, instrument making, and especially mapmaking.

New Amsterdam

*T*he Spanish hold on the Americas was so strong that attempts by the Dutch West India Company to set up trading posts were generally unsuccessful—with one remarkable exception. After his 1609 journey to North America, Henry Hudson described a well-sited harbor that offered protected anchorage. The Dutch West India Company decided to set up a trading post on the island that dominated the harbor—Manhattan Island.

By 1626 the Dutch had established the settlement of New Amsterdam, and in May, Peter Minuit negotiated with Mahican and Lenape Indians the purchase of Manhattan Island for a mere sixty guilders (then worth around twenty-four dollars). In 1664 a British fleet sent by James, duke of York, took control of the settlement. New Amsterdam was renamed New York in James's honor.

Gerardus Mercator (1512–1594), the first cartographer to give the name *atlas* to a book of maps, developed a map projection on which any straight line was a line of constant bearing. This feature made it far easier for navigators to plot ocean routes. The Mercator projection was crucial to the success of countless voyages of exploration. Abraham Ortelius (1527–1598) based his *Theatrum Orbis Terrarum* on eighty-seven sources, including Mercator. By 1612 over 7,300 copies had been printed in seven languages. In 1604 Jodocus Hondius (1563–1612) combined Mercator's original plates with his own maps. Owing to the immense popularity of his work, Hondius had the plates reengraved in miniature and issued under the title *Atlas Minor*.

SEE ALSO

NORDENSKIÖLD, NILS ADOLF ERIK

THE SWEDISH GEOLOGIST and explorer Nils Adolf Erik Nordenskiöld (1832–1901) made nine expeditions to the Arctic. On a voyage that lasted from 1878 to 1879 he became the first explorer to sail through the Northeast Passage, a direct sea route from Europe to Asia over northern Russia. In making this journey, Nordenskiöld attained one of the great goals of exploration.

Below **Nordenskiöld in 1895, five years after his final expedition.**

SCIENTIST AND EXPLORER

Nils Adolf Erik Nordenskiöld (usually known as Adolf) was born in Helsinki, the capital of Finland. Adolf's father was a leading figure in the field of mineralogy, the science concerned with minerals. Adolf shared his father's interests and studied mineralogy and chemistry at the University of Helsinki. While still a student, he accompanied his father on an expedition to the Ural Mountains in western Russia, where father and son studied the rich copper and iron mines.

In 1858 Nordenskiöld moved to Sweden (he later became a Swedish citizen) and was employed as a mineralogist at the National Museum in Stockholm. In 1858 and again in 1861 he served as a scientist on two expeditions commanded by Otto Torell, a geologist, to the island of Spitsbergen, part of the Svalbard archipelago deep inside the Arctic Circle. In 1864 Nordenskiöld led his own Spitsbergen expedition, and in 1868, as part of the Swedish North Polar Expedition, he reached a latitude of 81°42′ N and was awarded a gold medal by the British Royal Geographical Society for his achievement. In 1870 he explored the ice cap of western Greenland with huskies. Two years later, on another expedition to the North Pole, he was forced to spend the winter in Spitsbergen when his ship became trapped in the ice.

Above **Nordenskiöld's ship, the *Vega*, pictured trapped in the ice during the long dark winter of 1878/1879.**

Scientific study was the chief purpose of Nordenskiöld's expeditions. He plotted the height of mountains, collected fossils and geological specimens, studied ocean currents and the earth's magnetic field, and recorded the customs of the native peoples of the Arctic.

THE NORTHEAST PASSAGE

In 1875 and 1876 Nordenskiöld made two voyages to explore the Russian coast as far east as the Yenisei River, one of Siberia's great waterways, and became convinced that there was a navigable northeast passage. He felt that such a route would have practical benefits, for it would link the ports of northern Scandinavia with the mouth of several Siberian rivers and with the Pacific. Even if he was mistaken, the quest was worth the effort. Nordenskiöld wrote, "Every mile beyond the mouth of the Yenisei is a step forward to a complete knowledge of our globe."

NOVEMBER 18, 1832
Adolf Nordenskiöld is born in Finland.

1858–1861
Takes part in two expeditions to Spitsbergen led by Otto Torell.

1864
Leads his own scientific expedition to Spitsbergen.

1868
Takes part in the first Swedish North Polar Expedition.

1870
Using huskies, explores the interior of Greenland.

1872–1873
Attempting to reach the North Pole, becomes trapped in ice off Spitsbergen.

1875–1876
Makes two expeditions into the Russian Arctic and reaches the Yenisei River.

JULY 21, 1878
Sails from Norway in the *Vega*, aiming to complete the Northeast Passage.

SEPTEMBER 28, 1878
The *Vega* is stopped by ice.

The day before the *Vega* was frozen in, Nordenskiöld and his crew sat around a blazing fire on the shore and looked forward to reaching the warm waters of the Pacific:

We remained . . . chatting merrily about the remaining part of the voyage in seas where not cold but heat would trouble us. . . . None of us then had any idea that, instead of the heat of the tropics, we would for the next ten months be experiencing a winter at the pole of cold, frozen in on an unexpected road, under almost continual snowstorms, and with a temperature which often sank below the freezing point of mercury.

Nils Adolf Erik Nordenskiöld,
The Voyage of the Vega

VOYAGE OF THE *VEGA*

With support from Oscar II, king of Sweden and Norway, and funds from a wealthy Russian merchant, Nordenskiöld hired the *Vega*, a steam-powered whaling ship that was also equipped with sails. On July 21, 1878, the *Vega* set sail from the Arctic port of Tromsø, in northwestern Norway. The summer of 1878 was warm, and despite frequent stops for scientific observations, the *Vega* made good progress across the seas to the north of Russia. Yet just a short distance from the Pacific, on September 28 the *Vega*'s route was blocked by freshly formed sea ice. Nordenskiöld could see ice-free water ahead of him and was bitterly disappointed. He realized that, if he had arrived a few hours earlier, he would have managed to pass. He later wrote, "This misfortune of being frozen in so near my goal is the one mishap during all my Arctic journeys that I have had most difficulty in reconciling myself to."

JULY 18, 1879
The ice melts, and the ship is freed.

JULY 20, 1879
Nordenskiöld reaches the Pacific.

1881
Back in Sweden, publishes *The Voyage of the Vega*.

1882–1887
Publishes scientific report of the *Vega* voyage in five volumes.

1882–1883
Leads second expedition to the interior of western Greenland.

1890
Takes part in final Spitsbergen expedition.

1901
Dies in Sweden.

In a speech to the Swedish government, Nordenskiöld explained his aims in attempting the Northeast Passage:

I consider it probable that a well-equipped steamer would be able, without meeting too many obstacles from ice, to force a passage this way during autumn in a few days, and thus it would be possible not only to solve a geographical problem of several centuries' standing but also, with all the means now at the disposal of a man of science . . . to survey a hitherto almost unknown sea of enormous extent.

Below **Nordenskiöld studied the customs of the Greenland Inuit, shown hunting walrus in this 1845 painting.**

Nordenskiöld and his men had no option but to spend the next ten months on their trapped ship. Finally, on July 18, 1879, the ship was freed, and just two days later, on July 20, the *Vega* steamed triumphantly into the Pacific. The Northeast Passage had been navigated at last.

Back in Sweden, Nordenskiöld was made a baron in recognition of his achievement. He made a second expedition into the interior of Greenland in 1882 and 1883 and visited Spitsbergen for a sixth and final time in 1890.

In later years Nordenskiöld was acknowledged as the world's leading authority on polar exploration. Younger explorers, including the Norwegian Fridtjof Nansen, came to Nordenskiöld for advice and encouragement. Nordenskiöld also wrote several books, the most popular of which was *The Voyage of the Vega* (1881), an account of his famous journey.

SEE ALSO

- Bering, Vitus Jonassen • Cabot, Sebastian
- Nansen, Fridtjof • Northeast Passage
- Polar Exploration • Scandinavia

NORTHEAST PASSAGE

A DIRECT SEA ROUTE FROM EUROPE TO EAST ASIA was one of the most highly prized goals of European nations from the fifteenth century onward. With the treacherous southern ocean routes under the control of Spain and Portugal, the nations of northern Europe began to search for routes to the north. While many believed the best way lay to the northwest, across or around America, some maintained that a route lay to the northeast, through the Russian Arctic. After scores of fruitless attempts, the Northeast Passage was finally navigated by Nils Adolf Erik Nordenskiöld in 1879.

Left **On this French map, engraved in copper in about 1618, narrow sea passages, both to the northeast and to the northwest, connect Europe with Asia.**

NORTHERN ROUTES

The idea of trying to reach Asia by sailing north was suggested as early as 1527 by Robert Thorne, an English merchant living in Spain. In a letter to King Henry VIII, Thorne described the great wealth that the Spanish and Portuguese were bringing back from eastern Asia and the Pacific. However, Thorne noted the great distance traveled by the Spanish (who sailed around Cape Horn at the southern tip of South America) and the Portuguese (whose route took them around the Cape of Good Hope at Africa's southern tip). Thorne advised the king that a route to the north would be "a much shorter way than either the Spaniards or the Portuguese have."

ENGLISH VOYAGES

The first English attempt at a northeast passage was made in 1553. The Italian-born explorer Sebastian Cabot had set up the Company of Merchant Adventurers in London with the aim of opening up a trade route to China. Cabot commissioned an expedition to the northeast, to be commanded by Hugh Willoughby and Richard Chancellor.

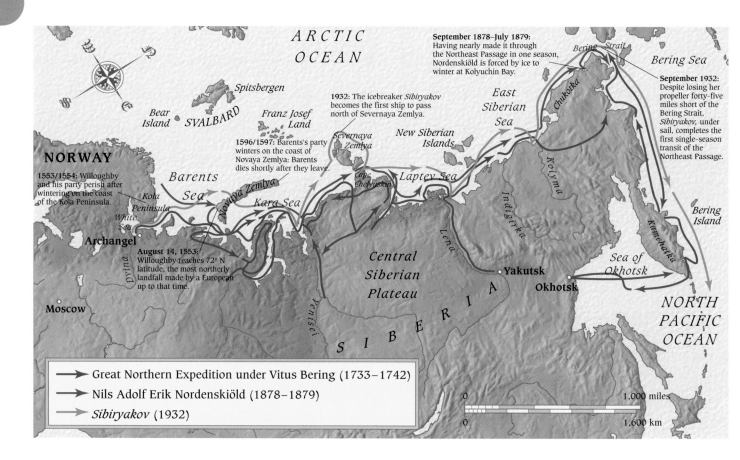

Map labels:

ARCTIC OCEAN

September 1878–July 1879: Having nearly made it through the Northeast Passage in one season, Nordenskiöld is forced by ice to winter at Kolyuchin Bay.

Bering Strait

Bering Sea

September 1932: Despite losing her propeller forty-five miles short of the Bering Strait, *Sibiryakov*, under sail, completes the first single-season transit of the Northeast Passage.

Spitsbergen

Bear Island

SVALBARD

Franz Josef Land

1932: The icebreaker *Sibiryakov* becomes the first ship to pass north of Severnaya Zemlya.

Severnaya Zemlya

East Siberian Sea

New Siberian Islands

Chukotka

1596/1597: Barents's party winters on the coast of Novaya Zemlya: Barents dies shortly after they leave.

NORWAY

Barents Sea

1553/1554: Willoughby and his party perish after wintering on the coast of the Kola Peninsula.

Kola Peninsula

White Sea

Novaya Zemlya

Kara Sea

Cape Chelyuskin

Laptev Sea

Kolyma

Indigirka

Bering Island

Archangel

August 14, 1553: Willoughby reaches 72° N latitude, the most northerly landfall made by a European up to that time.

Dvina

Yenisei

Lena

Central Siberian Plateau

Yakutsk

Okhotsk

Sea of Okhotsk

Kamchatka

Moscow

S I B E R I A

NORTH PACIFIC OCEAN

Legend:
→ Great Northern Expedition under Vitus Bering (1733–1742)
→ Nils Adolf Erik Nordenskiöld (1878–1879)
→ *Sibiryakov* (1932)

0   1,000 miles
0   1,600 km

Above **After almost four hundred years of failed attempts to find a navigable northeast passage, the first one-season transit of the whole route (generally known as the Northern Sea Route) was finally achieved by the Russian icebreaker *Sibiryakov* in 1932.**

After rounding northern Norway, the two men were separated by a storm. Willoughby was blown east to the island of Novaya Zemlya, from where he sailed west to the Kola Peninsula. Willoughby decided to spend the winter there, but long before spring, he and all of his men perished from the effects of cold, starvation, and scurvy.

Meanwhile, Richard Chancellor had reached the mouth of the Dvina River, on the northeastern coast of Russia. He traveled one thousand miles overland to Moscow and was welcomed at the court of Czar Ivan IV (known

as Ivan the Terrible). Upon returning to England, Chancellor reported to Cabot's company. Despite failing to find the passage, he had gathered much information about northern Russia, and his voyage marked the beginning of the trading of English woolen cloth and guns for Russian furs.

DUTCH VOYAGES

The Dutch were the great rivals of the English in the early quest for a northeast passage. The sea between Lapland and Novaya Zemlya is named after one of the Netherlands' most

1553
Hugh Willoughby and Richard Chancellor search for a northeast passage.

1594
Willem Barents crosses the sea later named after him.

1596–1597
Barents spends the winter on Novaya Zemlya.

1608–1609
Henry Hudson makes two voyages northeast to Novaya Zemlya.

1619
Czar Michael forbids foreign ships to sail in the Russian Arctic.

1728
Vitus Bering discovers that America and Asia are separated by a waterway, later named the Bering Strait.

1733–1742
Bering's expedition maps the northern coast of Russia.

1878–1879
After a winter trapped in the ice, Nils Adolf Erik Nordenskiöld completes the Northeast Passage.

1932
A Soviet icebreaker, *Sibiryakov*, makes the first single-season voyage through the passage.

highly regarded explorers, Willem Barents (c. 1550–1597), who crossed it three times, in 1594, 1595, and 1596.

On his third voyage Barents sailed far to the north and discovered Bear Island and Spitsbergen (in the Svalbard archipelago), which would later become bases for Dutch and English whale-hunting expeditions. Barents then sailed around the northern tip of Novaya Zemlya and into the Kara Sea. When his ship became trapped by ice, he and his crew were forced to spend a winter in the Arctic. They built a shelter out of driftwood and killed polar bears, whose fat they used to light oil lamps. Barents, who had been suffering from scurvy, died on the voyage home.

THE SEARCH ABANDONED

In the early 1600s the English explorer Henry Hudson searched for a northern passage from Europe to Asia in several directions— north, northeast, and northwest. On his northeast voyages Hudson, like earlier explorers, found his route blocked by sea ice and concluded that no northeast passage existed.

In 1619 Czar Michael of Russia, unhappy at the presence of foreign ships in his waters, declared that they would no longer be allowed to enter the Kara Sea. This decision ended English and Dutch attempts to find a northeast passage.

A member of Barents's crew described the winter on Novaya Zemlya:

It was so extremely cold that the fire cast almost no heat . . . as we put our feet to the fire, we burnt our hose [stockings] before we could feel the heat. . . . If we had not sooner smelt them rather than felt them, we should have burned them completely away before we knew it.

Gerrit de Veer

Left **Willem Barents spent the winter of 1596/1597 on Novaya Zemlya. This engraving of his driftwood shelter was made by Gerrit de Veer, who was among Barents's party.**

RUSSIAN EXPLORATIONS

In 1724 Czar Peter I of Russia (known as Peter the Great) sent the Danish navigator Vitus Bering on an expedition to discover if Asia and America were joined by land. In 1728, after a long voyage north from Kamchatka, Bering's discovery that the Siberian coast turned to the west proved that America and Asia were two separate continents. In 1733 Bering was given command of the ten-thousand-strong Great Northern Expedition, the aim of which was to map the coast of Siberia. By the time Bering died in 1741, the year before the completion of the expedition, he had proved that there was indeed a northeast passage through to East Asia.

SUCCESS

The Northeast Passage was finally navigated in July 1879 by the Swedish explorer Nils Adolf Erik Nordenskiöld. He had almost completed the journey the previous September, when he found himself frozen in and was forced to spend ten months waiting for the ice to melt.

Icebreakers

*F*irst built by Russian shipbuilders during the late nineteenth century, icebreakers are designed to force their way through the Northeast Passage in a single season. Their special features include increased propulsion and steeply sloping bows, which enable them to wedge their way up onto thick ice and crack it with their weight. The hulls of icebreakers are wide—so that the ships may cut a wide passage through the ice—and reinforced, in order to withstand the battering they undergo on the journey.

Unlike the Northwest Passage (through the Canadian Arctic), which is too tricky to be of any practical benefit, the Northeast Passage proved to be a useful route and is still regularly used by Russian icebreakers.

SEE ALSO

- Bering, Vitus Jonassen • Cabot, Sebastian
- Hudson, Henry • Nordenskiöld, Nils Adolf Erik
- Northwest Passage

NORTHWEST PASSAGE

SCATTERED THROUGHOUT THE DEADLY MAZE of narrow, ice-choked channels of the Canadian Arctic are the bones of hundreds of explorers who lost their lives while searching for a northwest passage, a waterway across the north of the American continent that would join the Atlantic Ocean to the Pacific. Such a waterway, whose existence was first proposed in the sixteenth century, would connect northern Europe to Asia and give those who controlled it access to the lucrative trade in Asian luxuries. The search remained fruitless until 1854, when a route was found on foot. The first explorer to sail through the Northwest Passage was Roald Amundsen, who did so in 1905.

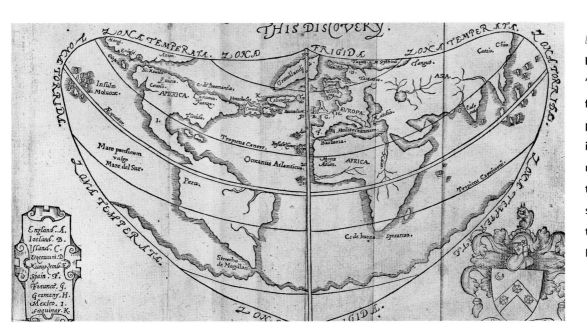

Left **This map, from Humphrey Gilbert's "Discourse," was the first world map to be printed in England and illustrated a short northwest passage in temperate latitudes. A short distance away lie the prized Molucca Islands.**

THE QUEST BEGINS

Within a few years of Christopher Columbus's 1492 voyage, it became clear that he had not reached Asia (as he thought). Instead, he had happened upon America, a continent previously unknown to Europeans and a barrier blocking the way to Asia. The goal of many explorers of the sixteenth century and after was to find a way through or around America.

EARLY ENGLISH VOYAGES

In 1576 Humphrey Gilbert, an English nobleman, published an essay ("Discourse") in which he argued that the shortest route from England to Asia lay to the northwest. Gilbert's essay marked the start of a determined English effort to find the passage. Over the next forty years, English merchant companies sent more than a dozen expeditions into the Arctic. The earliest were commanded by Martin Frobisher (1535–1594). However, the search for the passage was temporarily forgotten when, in 1576, Frobisher found rocks on Baffin Island that he thought contained gold. By 1578 he had brought over one thousand tons (about 1 million kg) of the rocks back to England—only to discover that they were worthless iron pyrite (fool's gold).

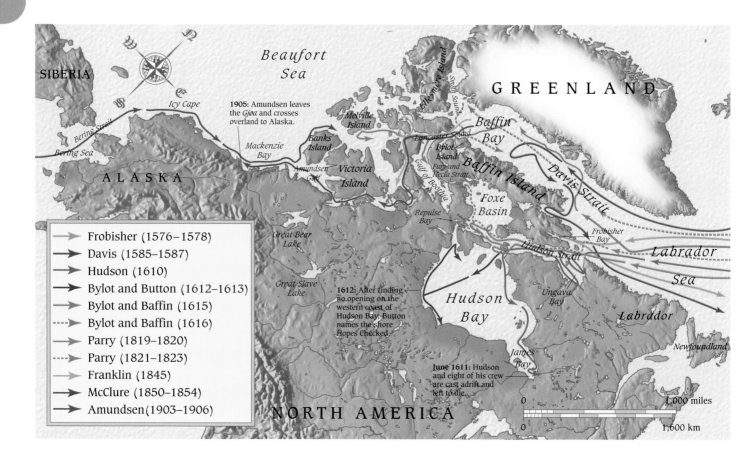

Above **The history of exploration of the Northwest Passage is characterized by false starts, wrong turnings, and tragedy. As it became clear that the Canadian Arctic offered no shortcut between the oceans (as earlier explorers had hoped), the achievement of finding the passage became an end in itself.**

Legend:
- Frobisher (1576–1578)
- Davis (1585–1587)
- Hudson (1610)
- Bylot and Button (1612–1613)
- Bylot and Baffin (1615)
- Bylot and Baffin (1616)
- Parry (1819–1820)
- Parry (1821–1823)
- Franklin (1845)
- McClure (1850–1854)
- Amundsen (1903–1906)

Map labels: SIBERIA; Beaufort Sea; GREENLAND; Icy Cape; 1905: Amundsen leaves the *Gjøa* and crosses overland to Alaska.; Bering Strait; Bering Sea; Melville Island; Baffin Bay; Banks Island; Lancaster Sound; Mackenzie Bay; Bylot Island; Ellesmere Island; Smith Sound; ALASKA; Amundsen Gulf; Victoria Island; Fury and Hecla Strait; Baffin Island; Davis Strait; Gulf of Boothia; Foxe Basin; Great Bear Lake; Repulse Bay; Frobisher Bay; Labrador Sea; Great Slave Lake; 1612: After finding no opening on the western coast of Hudson Bay, Button names the shore Hopes Checked.; Hudson Strait; Hudson Bay; Ungava Bay; Labrador; James Bay; Newfoundland; June 1611: Hudson and eight of his crew are cast adrift and left to die.; NORTH AMERICA; 0 — 1,000 miles; 0 — 1,600 km

In the 1580s the English navigator John Davis made three voyages to explore the strait that lies between Greenland and Baffin Island, later named Davis Strait in his honor. Davis was convinced that the passage lay at the top of this strait.

HUDSON BAY

In 1610, sailing west through the strait later named after him, Henry Hudson discovered a large sea, which he believed to be the Pacific. In fact, the sea was a huge bay (later named Hudson Bay). Hudson sailed south, but his ship became trapped in the ice at the foot of the bay. At the end of a punishing winter, his sick and exhausted crew mutinied. Hudson, his young son, and seven other crewmen were forced into the ship's boat and abandoned by the rest of the crew, who sailed home.

The mutineers escaped punishment by claiming that they knew how to find the Northwest Passage, which they said lay on the west side of Hudson Bay. In 1612 Robert Bylot, one of the mutineers, sailed back to Hudson Bay with Thomas Button. They explored the western coast of the bay but found no opening to the Pacific. Button named the shore Hopes Checked. In 1615 Bylot made another voyage, with the navigator William Baffin. The men explored Foxe Channel, to the north of Hudson Bay, but their passage was blocked by ice.

On their final voyage in 1616, Bylot and Baffin sailed up Davis Strait and discovered the bay later named after Baffin. Although they found an opening to the west, to which they gave the name Lancaster Sound, Baffin decided that there was no Northwest Passage. (As it happened, Lancaster Sound later turned out to be the entrance to the Northwest Passage.) On two separate explorations of Hudson Bay in 1631, Luke Foxe and Thomas James both concluded that no Northwest Passage existed. The search was abandoned.

William Parry 1790–1855

The English naval officer William Parry made three attempts to find the Northwest Passage. On his first, in 1819 and 1820, he sailed through Lancaster Sound and discovered and named Melville Island. He spent the winter there and kept his men entertained by staging theatrical performances. On a second voyage (1821–1823) he reached Fury and Hecla Strait, which he named after his ships. His third voyage ended in 1825 when one of his ships, the *Fury,* was wrecked and he was forced to return home. Parry's fourth and last expedition, in 1827, was an unsuccessful attempt to reach the North Pole by sled boat.

BRITISH NAVAL EXPEDITIONS

In 1815, after a long period of war with France, the British navy needed to find a new role for its ships and men. It was decided to send them on voyages of exploration, with the location of the Northwest Passage once again a major objective. Although hopes of a viable trading route had been abandoned, exploration, the quest for knowledge about the world, had become an end in itself.

From 1818 until 1845, the Royal Navy sent out numerous expeditions to explore the Canadian Arctic from both sides. Meanwhile, the English Hudson's Bay Company, which traded in Canadian furs, was sending explorers to the Arctic overland from the south.

The best-equipped British expedition was the third voyage of John Franklin, who sailed from England in 1845. Franklin encountered two whaling ships off the coast of Greenland; one of the whalers' captains reported that all the men were in high spirits. Franklin and his men, however, were never heard from again.

Right **This illustration, from William Parry's journal of his third voyage to the North American Arctic, depicts the wreck of the *Fury* on August 1, 1825, when the ship was driven ashore by an iceberg. As a consequence, Parry was forced to abandon his search for the Northwest Passage.**

Between 1848 and 1854, around forty search expeditions scoured the Arctic for signs of Franklin. In the process they mapped the course of more than one northwest passage. In 1854 one of the searchers, Robert McClure, became the first European to travel through a passage, partly on foot and by sled.

The Passage Conquered

The Norwegian explorer Roald Amundsen had read about the Franklin disaster as a boy and vowed to attempt the Northwest Passage himself. He learned to ski and served as an ordinary seaman on a seal-hunting expedition to the Arctic. From 1903 to 1906, in a converted herring fishing boat, the *Gjøa*, Amundsen made the first successful navigation of the passage, sailing from east to west.

Since Amundsen

Many ships have navigated the Northwest Passage since Amundsen's time. Even so, it is still too lengthy and difficult a voyage to be of practical benefit. In the early twenty-first century, however, as the earth's climate warms, less ice forms each year to block the passage. In 2002 scientists predicted that the

Right **On June 21, 1827, with the *Hecla* anchored in an ice harbor carved out by the crew in Spitsbergen, Parry set out for the Pole with twenty-two men, four sled boats, and enough food for seventy-one days.**

1576–1578
Martin Frobisher makes three voyages to Baffin Island.

1585–1587
On three voyages, John Davis explores the waterway later named Davis Strait.

1610–1611
Henry Hudson's voyage to Hudson Bay ends in his death.

1612
Robert Bylot and Thomas Button explore the west coast of Hudson Bay.

1615
Bylot and William Baffin explore Hudson Strait and Foxe Channel.

1616
Baffin and Bylot sail to the top of Davis Strait.

1631
Luke Foxe and Thomas James conclude independently that no passage exists.

1819–1820
William Parry sails through Lancaster Sound, which later proves to be the entrance to the passage.

1819–1822
John Franklin explores the north Canadian coast.

1821–1823
Parry sails through Hudson Strait to Fury and Hecla Strait.

1824–1825
Parry's third attempt to find a northwest passage ends with the wreck of his ship.

On the morning of August 26, 1906, Roald Amundsen was told that a ship had been sighted to the west:

I was woken by a tremendous running back and forth on deck . . . then Lieutenant Hanson burst into the cabin and shouted the unforgettable words, "Vessel in sight!" The North-West Passage was done. My boyhood dream—at that moment it was accomplished. A strange feeling welled up in my throat . . . it was weakness in me—but I felt tears in my eyes. "Vessel in sight" . . . "Vessel in sight."

Roald Amundsen, *The North West Passage*

Northwest Passage would be free of ice within fifty years and would thus be open at last as a regular shipping route. Though nothing can be certain where long-range weather predictions are involved, there is at least a chance that the dream of Frobisher, Davis, and Hudson may one day be fulfilled after all.

SEE ALSO

- Amundsen, Roald • Baffin, William
- Cabot, John • Cabot, Sebastian
- Franklin, John • Frobisher, Martin
- Hakluyt, Richard • Hudson, Henry
- Polar Exploration

1825–1827
Franklin embarks on his second expedition to the Canadian Arctic.

1837–1839
Peter Dease and Thomas Simpson of the Hudson's Bay Company map much of the Canadian Arctic coast.

1845
Franklin disappears with two ships while searching for the passage.

1848–1854
Forty expeditions search unsuccessfully for Franklin but survey most of the Canadian Arctic.

1854
Robert McClure completes the passage from west to east, partly on foot and by sled.

1905
Roald Amundsen sails through the passage—a feat unmatched for forty years.

1940–1944
The *Saint Roch,* a vessel belonging to the Royal Canadian Mounted Police, becomes the first ship to sail through the passage from west to east.

1954
The Canadian naval ship HMCS *Labrador* completes the passage.

1960
The U.S. Navy submarine *Seadragon* navigates the passage.

1969
The oil tanker *Manhattan* completes the passage.

NÚÑEZ DE BALBOA, VASCO

OF THE MANY FEATS OF EXPLORATION that have been commemorated in verse, the achievement of Vasco Núñez de Balboa (1475–1519) is perhaps the most famous. A Spanish soldier, governor, and explorer of new territories in Central America, Núñez de Balboa was the first European to set eyes on the Pacific. Núñez de Balboa possessed many characteristics common to the Spanish conquistadores who opened up the New World for Europeans in the sixteenth century: he was brave, debonair, and also capable of ruthlessness.

Right **Having crossed Panama from side to side, Núñez de Balboa took triumphant possession of the Pacific Ocean, named the Mar del Sur (South Sea) on this sixteenth-century Spanish engraving.**

CONQUISTADOR AND GOVERNOR

Born into a noble family in Badajoz or Jerez in southwestern Spain, Vasco Núñez de Balboa was twenty-five when he arrived in the New World to seek his fortune. After joining a voyage in search of pearls along the Caribbean coast of Colombia, he settled on the island of Hispaniola and tried his hand at farming. His attempt was unsuccessful, and pursued by creditors, in 1510 he fled the island, together with his dog Leoncico, hidden in a barrel aboard a resupply ship.

The ship was bound for the Gulf of Urabá (in present-day northwestern Colombia), where Balboa's knowledge of the area was of great value to the colonists. On his advice the settlement was transported to a more favorable base on the northern coast of the Isthmus of Panama, the narrow finger of land that connects North and South America. The new colony, Santa María la Antigua del Darién, prospered by the acquisition of local goods, through enforced trade with local people. Despite gaining a reputation for barbarity,

Núñez de Balboa became the colony's most popular figurehead and, in 1511, appointed himself governor of the settlement, which became known simply as Darién.

THE PACIFIC

While exploring the area around the settlement, Núñez de Balboa heard Indian stories of a great sea and a land of fabulous wealth (perhaps the kingdom of the Incas) to the south. On September 1, 1513, he set out with a team of 190 Europeans and 800 Indians,

Pedro Arias Dávila c. 1440–1531

Known to most of his contemporaries as Pedrarias, Pedro Arias Dávila was responsible for the foundation and administration of the Spanish colonies in Panama (1514) and Nicaragua (1516). He founded Panama City (1519) and supported Francisco Pizarro's expeditions into Peru in search of Incan gold. A former soldier, he was elderly (perhaps seventy-four) when he arrived in the New World in 1514. His quiet, meticulous methods were at odds with the impetuousness of the younger conquistadores, and there were frequent disagreements between Dávila and Núñez de Balboa.

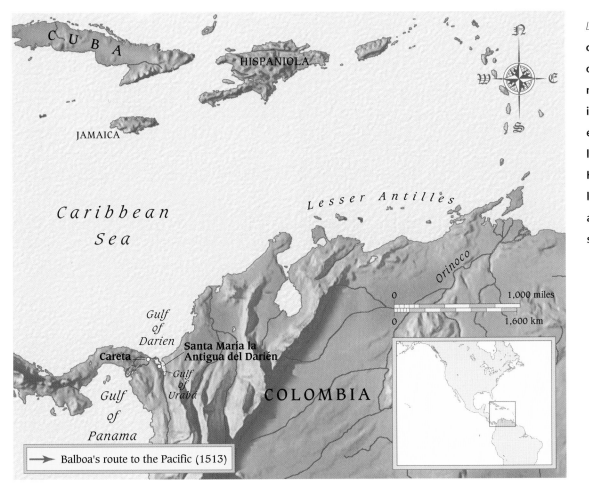

Left **Núñez de Balboa's crossing of the Isthmus of Panama, one of the most significant events in the history of exploration, took a little over three weeks. He assumed that Asia lay a short distance away over a narrow stretch of water.**

→ Balboa's route to the Pacific (1513)

1475
Vasco Núñez de Balboa is born in Spain.

1501
Explores Caribbean coast of South America in search of gold and pearls.

1502–1510
Settles on Hispaniola.

1511
Appoints himself governor of Darién.

SEPTEMBER 25, 1513
Becomes the first European to see the Pacific Ocean from its eastern shore.

1514
Returns to Darién. Pedro Arias Dávila arrives in Darién.

1516–1518
Núñez de Balboa explores the Gulf of Panama.

1519
After a trial, is executed for treason, with four others, at Acla.

dismantled ships across the isthmus, reassembled them on the Pacific coast, and explored the Gulf of Panama.

Dávila, fearing that he was being undermined in Núñez de Balboa's reports to Spain, plotted to get rid of his rival. He recalled Núñez de Balboa at the end of 1518 and found him guilty on a number of charges, including treason, rebellion, and maltreatment of native peoples. Núñez de Balboa was beheaded on January 21, 1519.

LEGACY

Although Vasco Núñez de Balboa is remembered by many as a ruthless man, his sighting of the Pacific was an event of immense importance in the history of exploration. Christopher Columbus had died in 1506 firmly believing that he had reached the outlying islands of Japan and China. Although many of his contemporaries were sceptical, it was not until Núñez de Balboa's discovery of the Pacific that their suspicions were confirmed. That single act established the existence of the American continent and almost doubled the size of the known world.

SEE ALSO
• Spain

Above **Núñez de Balboa sighted the Pacific Ocean from a hilltop a few days before arriving at the Gulf of San Miguel.**

hoping to find the great ocean. He crossed the dense jungles and mountains of the Isthmus of Panama on foot and, standing on a hilltop on September 25, 1513, became the first European to see the Pacific Ocean from its eastern shore. Naming it the South Sea, he claimed the ocean and the surrounding coastal lands for Spain.

A new governor, Pedro Arias Dávila, reached Darién in June 1514, and from the outset, he and Núñez de Balboa did not get on. After much heated debate, Dávila agreed to let Núñez de Balboa return to the South Sea. In 1516 a small expedition party carried

OÑATE, JUAN DE

JUAN DE OÑATE (1550–1630) WAS THE FIRST PERSON of European descent to colonize what is now the southwestern United States. He explored the region of present-day New Mexico with great vigor and determination and established the first Spanish settlements there. Like many conquistadores of the sixteenth century, Oñate could be ruthless; he was driven as much by a desire for wealth and prestige as by missionary zeal or an interest in geographical exploration.

GENTLEMAN OF THE NEW WORLD

By the time Juan de Oñate reached adulthood, the Spanish had strengthened their hold over the colony of New Spain (present-day Mexico), and life for the colonizers was settling down. Yet to the north, beyond an uncertain frontier, lay vast unmapped lands. Inhabited by various Indian tribes, these lands were virtually unknown to the European colonizers of the Americas. According to a number of rumors that circulated at the time, fantastic wealth was to be found in cities of gold that lay in the uncharted territory.

When he decided to test the truth of the rumors, Juan de Oñate was already very wealthy. The owner of silver mines in Zacatecas, he was said to be the richest man in New Spain. His prestige had been further enhanced by his marriage to Isabel de Tolosa Cortés, the granddaughter of Hernán Cortés, the esteemed vanquisher of the Aztecs and conqueror of New Spain. Why so well-favored a man as Oñate chose, in his late forties, to give up his life of ease and head north remains unclear. He may have been prompted by a desire to see his own name alongside

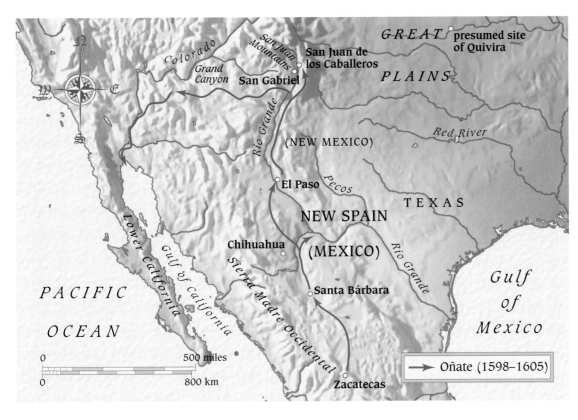

Left **Juan de Oñate pioneered a route north from New Spain that served Spanish traders, settlers, and missionaries until the end of the nineteenth century. It became known as the Camino Real de Tierra Adentro (royal road to the interior lands), or simply, the Camino Real.**

that of his wife's illustrious ancestor in the chronicles of Spanish conquest.

El Paso

In 1595 the Spanish government gave Oñate permission to venture north on an expedition that he undertook to fund himself. The idea of forming a new colony had widespread appeal; it took almost three years to assemble and organize all those who wished to take part. When the expedition eventually left, it made a dramatic sight. The four-mile-long caravan comprised eighty-three wagons, over seven thousand horses and other animals, and around five hundred settlers, soldiers, priests, slaves, and guides. The procession snaked out of the frontier settlement of Santa Bárbara in January 1598.

After traveling for three months in the near-desert terrain, Oñate and his expedition were met by Manso Indians. The Manso proved to be friendly and showed the settlers across the Rio Grande. Oñate named the place where they crossed the river El Paso del Rio del Norte (the ford of the river of the north), a name that was soon simplified to its modern-day form, El Paso. Once across the river, the expedition paused and observed a general thanksgiving. Part of the ceremony included the performance of a special play, *La Toma* (The taking); this play signified the official acquisition of New Mexico for the king of Spain.

1550
Juan de Oñate is born in New Spain.

1595
Is granted permission to settle territories to the north of New Spain.

1598
Expedition sets out; San Juan and San Gabriel are founded.

1601
Oñate searches in vain for treasure of Quivira.

1604–1605
Explores Colorado River and Gulf of California.

1607
Is replaced as governor of New Mexico by Don Pedro de Peralta.

1612
Is found guilty of various offenses committed during his time as governor.

1624
After several appeals, is acquitted.

1630
Dies.

Above **Walter Raleigh's 1595 map of the fabled land of El Dorado includes the mythical sacrificial lake. Indian legend told of a chief ritually dusted with gold before being washed in the lake.**

The Quivira Treasure

Oñate was as obsessed with treasure as many conquistadores before him had been. Spanish explorers in South America were enticed into launching a great many expeditions in search of El Dorado, a fabled land of infinite riches. The North American equivalent to El Dorado was Quivira, thought to have been situated near the Great Bend of the Arkansas River, in present-day central Kansas. Its existence had first been mentioned to Francisco Vásquez de Coronado (c. 1510–1554) by an Indian whom he named the Turk. The Turk reported that at Quivira, ordinary pots and pans were made of gold. Just as Coronado had done sixty years earlier, Oñate searched for the fabulous riches of Quivira—and found nothing.

DISGRACE

It soon transpired that different members of Oñate's expedition party had different reasons for participating in the expedition. The settlers had come seeking fresher and richer pastures than those of New Spain; when they did not find them, they wished to return home. The priests wanted to pursue their missionary work among the Indians. Oñate and his soldiers—who acted as a kind of police force—were seeking fame, power, and wealth. The Spaniards' treatment of any native peoples who resisted the invasion of their land was often harsh. After one attack on Oñate's party, a whole Indian village was virtually wiped out as a reprisal. The priests objected vociferously and wrote letters to New Spain recommending that the new colony be abandoned.

In present-day New Mexico, Oñate established a temporary base at San Juan de los Caballeros, where the Rio Grande meets with the Rio Chama, while a permanent settlement was built at San Gabriel. Search parties were sent out to look for silver. When none was found, Oñate maintained order among the settlers by executing some of the leaders. In 1601 he headed north himself with a hand-picked band to hunt for the treasure of Quivira. When he returned empty handed at the end of the year, he found that most of the settlers had gone home.

In 1604 Oñate embarked on one last desperate quest for silver. First he went west to the Colorado River, and then he continued south to the Gulf of California. Yet again, he returned poorer than he had set out. He was forced to resign his post as governor of New Mexico and was later tried on charges of cruelty, immorality, and false reporting. He won his appeal against the verdict, but his reputation was ruined.

REPUTATION RESTORED

Although the court was unable to restore Oñate's reputation, history did so. He is favorably remembered in the southwestern United States as a founding father, the man who crossed the Rio Grande and established the first inland European settlement in North America. His exploration, which took him as far as Kansas in the north and California in the west, was indeed pioneering and considerably extended European knowledge of the area.

Right **The discovery of golden artifacts lent force to rumors of El Dorado. Dredged up from Lake Siecha in present-day Colombia, this raft appears to depict a ritual sacrifice.**

The First Thanksgiving?

*T*he traditional American ceremony of Thanksgiving is generally considered to date from 1621, when the Pilgrim Fathers, Puritans who established the first permanent colony in New England, joined with local Indians to give thanks for their first harvest. Captain Gasper Perez de Villagra, who traveled with Oñate and described his own experiences in his *History of New Mexico,* suggested an earlier beginning. On reaching the Rio Grande in April 1598, Oñate's trekkers paused and gave thanks to God for their safe arrival. Some see this ceremony as the first true American Thanksgiving.

SEE ALSO

• Coronado, Francisco Vásquez de
• Cortés, Hernán

OTHERWORLDS

THE IMAGINATION IS A BOUNDLESS TERRITORY. In a story an explorer may go anywhere imaginable by any means imaginable. Since the earliest times people have told stories of journeys to mythical otherworlds, whether on earth, under the sea, or in space. Many such stories were inspired by real voyages, but in some cases real voyages were inspired by the stories. Fictional adventurers reached Brazil and the moon, for example, long before real adventurers did.

Below **Jason's *Argo* was almost crushed by the Symplegades, or clashing rocks, which may correspond to the narrow passage that connects the Bosporus with the Black Sea.**

MYTH AND MIGRATION

Many ancient Greek otherworld myths are thought to have a historical basis. In one story Jason and a band of heroes sail aboard the *Argo* through an array of mythical lands where they encounter snakes, dragons, and many other fantastical (and often brutal) creatures. The story may be a retelling of Greek expeditions to conquer and colonize lands around the Black Sea. Homer's *Odyssey* (c. 800 BCE), tells of the wanderings of Odysseus around the Mediterranean—a journey taken by many Greek-speaking peoples as Greek influence spread. Stories of the Trojan War, most notably Homer's *Iliad*, despite elements of fantasy, may record a migration of Greek-speaking peoples to the area of Troy.

VOYAGES BY SEA

Otherworld myths often involve their heroes in voyages across the sea. In a popular tale from *The Thousand and One Nights*, a collection of eastern stories dating from the eighth century onward, Sindbad the Sailor tells of seven voyages on which he narrowly escaped danger in various fantastical lands. Sindbad's stories were almost certainly based on the experiences of merchants from Basra (in Iraq), who sailed to eastern Asia to trade. Similarly, in the fourteenth-century *Travels of Sir John Mandeville*, accounts of real places are embelished with elements of myth and fantasy.

PRESTER JOHN

The lands visited by Sir John Mandeville (whose identity is uncertain) included the realm of Prester John, a legendary Christian priest-king whose armies were said to have inflicted several defeats on Muslim kings of central Asia. As stories of Prester John interwove historical people, places, and events and as they gave European Christians hope of an ally in their battles to oust Muslims from the Holy Land, there was a persistent belief in Europe that Prester John really existed. Several expeditions were sent to eastern Asia, and when they failed to locate Prester John (but in the process established trade contact with the Mongol Empire), the focus shifted to East Africa. Portuguese exploration of Africa during the fifteenth century was inspired, in part, by the desire to find Prester John.

OTHERWORLDS ON MEDIEVAL MAPS

The enlargement of the known world, in particular, the discovery of outlying regions of the Americas in the sixteenth century, inspired much speculation about what explorers might find, expressed vividly in maps of the period. The interior of South America, for instance, was often filled with images of fearsome creatures and savage cannibals.

Left **This depiction of Sindbad embarking is taken from a nineteenth-century French edition of *The Thousand and One Nights.***

c. 800 BCE
Stories of Jason and the Argonauts are in circulation; Homer composes the *Iliad* and the *Odyssey*.

c. 150 CE
Lucian of Samosata writes his *True History*.

987
The first tales of *The Thousand and One Nights* are collated.

c. 1356
The Voyage and Travels of Sir John Mandeville is published.

1516
Thomas More's *Utopia* is published.

1726
Jonathan Swift's *Gulliver's Travels* is published.

1863
Jules Verne publishes the first of his novels describing an extraordinary journey.

1896
H. G. Wells publishes *The Island of Dr. Moreau*.

1902
Georges Méliès produces one of the first films, *Le voyage dans la lune*.

1932
Aldous Huxley's *Brave New World* is published.

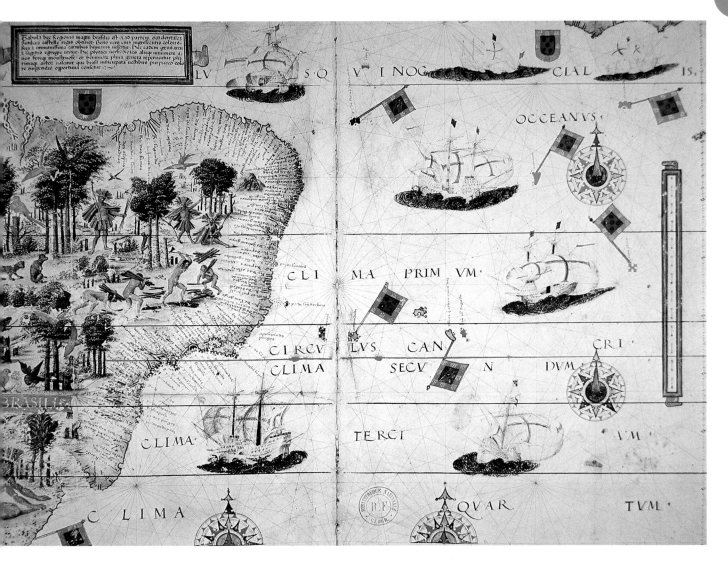

Certain mythical otherworlds recur on medieval maps. One is the island of Atlantis, first described by the ancient Greek philosopher Plato. Atlantis was said to have been swallowed up by the sea after its citizens defied the gods. There was a widespread belief in medieval Europe that Atlantis lay somewhere in (or under) the Atlantic Ocean, and many explorers had the real hope that they might find it. The mythical Southern Continent (*Terra Australis*) appears on a great many medieval maps, and numerous voyages were launched in the hope of locating it. During the sixteenth century, rumors persisted of cities of gold somewhere in the Americas. Such rumors seemed to be confirmed by native reports, and huge efforts were expended by Spaniards searching for the mythical golden cities of El Dorado, Cibola, and Quivira. While no such cities were found, the expeditions led to the exploration and conquest of vast new territories.

Above **Proud peoples and exotic animals fill the interior of Brazil on this 1519 map.**

After a shipwreck Lemuel Gulliver, the hero of *Gulliver's Travels* (1726), finds himself washed up on an island somewhere in the South Pacific. After a deep sleep he wakes up:

I attempted to rise, but was not able to stir: for as I happened to lie on my back, I found my arms and legs were strongly fastened to the ground; and my hair, which was long and thick, tied down in the same manner. . . . In a little time I felt something alive moving on my left leg, which advancing gently forward over my breast, came almost up to my chin; when bending mine eyes downwards as much as I could, I perceived it to be a human creature not six inches high . . .

Jonathan Swift, *Gulliver's Travels*

DESERT ISLANDS

The discovery and exploration of the vast, island-speckled Pacific in the seventeenth and eighteenth centuries inspired a great many stories that place otherworlds on desert islands. The idea common to many such stories is that the battle for survival on an isolated island, far from the trappings of civilization and the structures of society, reveals the essence of a person. In some cases, notably William Golding's *Lord of the Flies* (1954), human nature is revealed to be savage. On the other hand, J. M. Ballantyne's *The Coral Island* (1858) shows people marooned on an island to be courageous, good-natured, and resourceful. In Daniel Defoe's *Robinson Crusoe* (1719), the hero survives through a combination of spiritual resolve and physical ingenuity. Defoe based his story on the real-life adventures of the Scottish sailor Alexander Selkirk, marooned from 1704 to 1709 on an island four hundred miles (640 km) west of Chile. Despite nearly going mad with loneliness, Selkirk managed to survive by eating fruit and goat's meat and by taming cats to keep rats at bay.

Jules Verne *1828–1905*

*T*he immensely popular French novelist Jules Verne wrote over fifty novels. Many describe fantastical voyages, including *A Journey to the Center of the Earth* (written in 1864), *From the Earth to the Moon* (1865), and *Twenty Thousand Leagues under the Sea* (1870).

Remarkably, Verne's novels described submarines, automobiles, and vehicles for space travel many years before they had been invented. Verne was a scrupulous researcher who based all his inventions on the very latest scientific information and imagined only what the engineers of his day might be capable of building. Successful science fiction presents an alternative reality that strikes the reader as being within the bounds of possibility, not one that is entirely fantastical. It is for this reason that Jules Verne is considered the father of the genre.

UTOPIAS AND DYSTOPIAS

Plato's *Republic* (written in the early fourth century BCE) was the first of a number of literary works to portray a mythical ideal society. In his 1516 work *Utopia*, Thomas More describes an island state, perhaps based on lands reported by Amerigo Vespucci, where gold is despised and people live communally. Although the title of his work came to designate any ideal world, More is not unreserved in his praise of life in Utopia. The legend of the lost island of Atlantis inspired many more island utopias.

The term *dystopia*, coined in the nineteenth century, denotes the opposite of a utopian society, that is, one where social structures have in some sense broken down. In H. G. Wells's *The Island of Doctor Moreau* (1896), the hero finds himself shipwrecked on an island presided over by a sadistic doctor. In Jonathan Swift's *Gulliver's Travels* (1726), Lemuel Gulliver sails to a number of dysfunctional otherworlds, including Lilliput, a land inhabited by self-important little people who wage wars over trivial matters, and Laputa, whose high-minded intellectuals are too self-absorbed to deal with everyday matters. Swift's otherworlds, like many dystopias, offer satiric comment on the shortcomings of the real world.

OTHERWORLDS OF THE FUTURE

Twentieth-century literature offers several examples of dystopian otherworlds separated from the real world not by mountains or seas but by time. Aldous Huxley's *Brave New World* (set in the twenty-sixth century and published in 1932), George Orwell's *1984* (set in what was then the near future and published in 1948), and Ray Bradbury's *Fahrenheit 451* (set in the twenty-fourth century and published in 1953) all portray the consequences of the deprivation of human liberty by totalitarian regimes.

Above This map of the mythical island of Utopia, the frontispiece to a 1518 edition of Thomas More's work, was engraved by Ambrosius Holbein. The fictional traveler Raphael Hythloday (who has seen much of the world while voyaging with Amerigo Vespucci) describes the happy island state, where food is owned communally and value is placed only on goods that are useful—thus, gold and silver are not stored in vaults but used to make chamber pots and stools.

Above **This illustration of a moon landing formed the frontispiece to an 1890 edition of Jules Verne's novel *Autour de la lune* (*Around the Moon*).**

supremacy. Popularized in a great number of comic books, television programs, and block-buster movies, science fiction also achieved literary recognition with the works of writers such as Isaac Asimov, Ray Bradbury, Arthur C. Clarke, and Robert Heinlein. It will be several decades, at least, before real explorers finally prove or disprove the existence of extraterrestrial otherworlds.

The Man in the Moon

The earliest fictional account of lunar life is found in the *True History* of Lucian of Samosata (c. 120–c. 180 CE), in which a group of sailors are propelled up to the moon by a giant waterspout. When Galileo made the first lunar observations with a telescope in 1609, his discovery that the surface was marked by mountains, valleys, and plains lent force to arguments for the existence of lunar peoples. The Polish astronomer Johannes Hevelius (1611–1687) drew detailed maps of the moon's surface and gave the name Selenites to the people he believed lived there.

Despite the accumulation of evidence in the nineteenth century that the moon lacked both the air and water necessary to support life, pro-Selenite theories abounded. One of the first cinematic films was Georges Méliès's 1902 work *Le voyage dans la lune* (*Trip to the Moon*). In 1969 the first manned lunar landing finally proved that the moon lacked inhabitants.

THE FINAL FRONTIER

During the twentieth century, as the position of the earth within a system of planets became more clearly understood, the spirit of exploration, conquest, and adventure was to a certain extent reawakened. In many science fiction stories, the Age of Discovery is reimagined on a cosmic scale. Intrepid explorers venture into space, and the inhabitants of extraterrestrial otherworlds vie for military

SEE ALSO
- Dampier, William • Mapmaking
- Southern Continent • Space Exploration

PARK, MUNGO

MUNGO PARK, BORN IN SCOTLAND IN 1771, made two expeditions into the interior of West Africa to establish the true course of the Niger River. The West African interior was relatively unexplored at that time, and Park suffered great hardship. In 1806, during his second mission, he and his companions drowned in the Niger, apparently after coming under attack.

Mungo Park was the seventh of thirteen children born to a Scottish farmer. Despite his humble background, he was well educated and studied medicine at Edinburgh University. In 1792 he took a post as assistant to the ship's surgeon on a voyage to Indonesia. Park became fascinated by the natural history of the island of Sumatra. Upon his return to London in 1794, he gave lectures about the fascinating animals and plants he had seen. Though he was only twenty-three years old, Park's enthusiasm and talent caught the eye of Sir Joseph Banks, the founder of the African Association.

THE RACE TO TIMBUKTU

The African Association had been founded in 1788 to finance expeditions to the African interior, which was little known and held the promise of untapped sources of wealth. Since the early Middle Ages, Islamic travelers had circulated stories about a place they called Timbuktu, a fabled city of gold that was reported to lie a short distance from the banks of the Niger River.

SEPTEMBER 10, 1771
Mungo Park is born at Foulshiels, Scotland.

1792
Travels to Sumatra.

1795
Sets off on first expedition to reach the Niger River from the West African coast.

1797
Returns to Britain.

1799
Publishes *Travels into the Interior of Africa;* marries and returns to Scotland.

1805
Returns to Africa to complete his exploration of the Niger River.

1806
Dies at Bussa (in present-day Nigeria).

Above **Park's hope of being the first explorer accurately to chart the course of the Niger River led to his death at the age of only thirty-five.**

Right **Many Europeans hoped that the Niger River would provide much-hoped-for access to the interior of Africa, especially to the city of Timbuktu, whose wealth was legendary (but vastly overstated). Park affirmed the eastward flow of the Niger but died attempting to reach its mouth.**

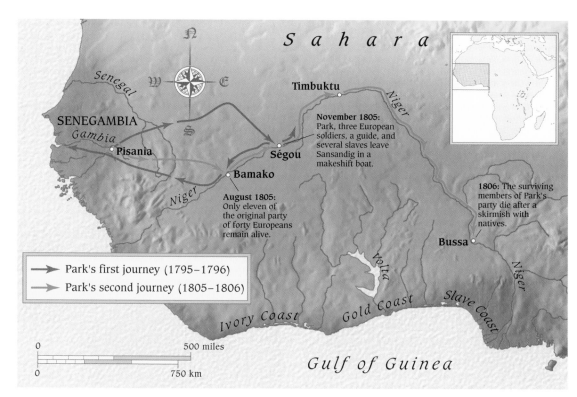

S a h a r a

Timbuktu

November 1805: Park, three European soldiers, a guide, and several slaves leave Sansandig in a makeshift boat.

SENEGAMBIA

Pisania

Ségou

Bamako

August 1805: Only eleven of the original party of forty Europeans remain alive.

1806: The surviving members of Park's party die after a skirmish with natives.

Bussa

→ Park's first journey (1795–1796)
→ Park's second journey (1805–1806)

Ivory Coast *Gold Coast* *Slave Coast*

0   500 miles
0   750 km

Gulf of Guinea

Although stories of Timbuktu (present-day Tombouctou in Mali) had reached Europe, by the 1790s no explorer had yet managed to travel there. In 1795 Banks approached Park on behalf of the African Association and offered to fund an expedition, which Park would lead, to find out as much as possible about the Niger River and to visit Timbuktu.

INTO THE JUNGLE

On May 22, 1795, Park set sail from Portsmouth in southern England, headed for the West African coast. Ahead of him lay many dangers, including navigating a route through unmapped areas of thick jungle and open desert, meeting unfamiliar native peoples, encountering wild animals, and risking death or serious illness from tropical diseases. Nevertheless, Park carried the bare minimum of equipment. He took a compass and a pocket sextant, and in his luggage were a couple of pairs of pistols, changes of linen, and tobacco and beads to trade with Africans.

Arriving at the African coast, Park sailed up the Gambia River. Two hundred miles (320 km)

inland, the river became unnavigable. Park proceeded by foot until he reached a small British camp at Pisania, where he remained for a few months to learn Mandingo, the local language, and to discover more about local culture. The next leg of his expedition was delayed when he contracted a mysterious fever that almost killed him.

By December 1795 Park was well enough to continue. He took two local guides, a horse, two asses, and enough food for two days. With these meager provisions, Park set off into the wilderness, only to meet a group of bandits, who took most of his tobacco.

AFRICAN TEST

Over the following two years, Park's perseverance was tested to the full, but Africa continued to thrill him, and he remained determined to reach the Niger. He met friendly people, who helped him by giving him food and shelter, as well as people who attacked and robbed him because of his skin color and his Christianity (many West African peoples were Muslims). His fate seemed most

When he returned to Britain, Park wrote a memoir of his travels in which he described the people who had kidnapped him in 1796.

All these ladies were remarkably corpulent, which is considered here as the highest mark of beauty. They were very inquisitive, and examined my hair and skin with great attention, but affected to consider me as a sort of inferior being to themselves, and would knit their brows, and seemed to shudder, when they looked at the whiteness of my skin.

Mungo Park,
Travels into the Interior of Africa

desperate when he was kidnapped and kept in a mud hut for a month. He was tortured and starved but, despite his weakness, managed to make a dramatic escape. Alone in the desert and half dead from exhaustion and dehydration, he rallied himself and continued his journey.

On July 21, 1796, Park finally arrived at Ségou, on the Niger River. Traveling around by canoe, he gathered information about the flow of the Niger and the various places he passed through. Following the river westward, he met more dangers, including a near-fatal encounter with a lion and another altercation with bandits. At Bamako, where he once again fell ill with a raging fever, he was finally forced to abandon his mission.

Below **In his *Travels into the Interior of Africa*, from which this illustration is taken, Park describes a bamboo bridge "of a very singular construction" that crossed the Bafing River, part of the Senegal River.**

René-Auguste Caillié *1799–1838*

*T*he first European to reach Timbuktu (present-day Tombouctou) and live to tell the story was the French explorer René-Auguste Caillié. Disguised as an Arab, in April 1828 he traveled alone from the West African coast along the Niger River to Timbuktu. Then he headed northward across the Sahara Desert to complete a remarkable 4,500-mile (7,240 km) journey.

RÉNÉ CAILLIÉ

Above **After a remarkable journey to Timbuktu in 1828, René Caillié found a far less prosperous city than Europeans had been expecting.**

Park returned to Britain in December 1797 to a hero's welcome. His account of his adventures, *Travels into the Interior of Africa* (1799), was enormously popular. Although Park toned down much of what had happened to him, many readers still found his stories stunning. Demonstrating his regard for African people, he wrote, "whatever difference there is between the negro and European … there is none in the genuine sympathies and characteristic feelings of our common nature."

LOST WITHOUT A TRACE

In 1799 Park married and settled in Peebles, Scotland. He practiced as a surgeon but always planned to return to Africa. On January 30, 1805, he set off with five thousand pounds and forty soldiers on a government-backed mission to establish an English settlement on the Niger.

By April, the expedition had reached Pisania, but as the rainy season started many of the men were struck down by fever. In August, Park and eleven survivors reached Bamako and began their journey eastward along the Niger. Park's last communications were letters written from Sansandig (north of Ségou) in November 1805. He left Sansandig with only three Europeans, a guide, and several slaves (one of whom survived to tell the tale). It appears that the men managed to sail one thousand miles downstream, repulsing native attacks all the way. When their boat became stuck on rocks at Bussa, in present-day Nigeria, Park and his companions faced a hail of arrows. They jumped into the river to save themselves and drowned.

SEE ALSO
• Banks, Joseph

PEARY, ROBERT E.

A WIRY, WEATHER-BEATEN MAN, the American explorer Robert Edwin Peary (1856–1920) is remembered for his tenacity and ambition as well as for his remarkable achievements in the field of Arctic exploration. Peary was less obviously charismatic than his fellow polar explorers Fridtjof Nansen and Robert Scott, but his resourcefulness in dealing with the challenges of polar weather and terrain was unsurpassed. His behavior toward the Inuit, the native inhabitants of the North American Arctic, was extremely generous and humane.

Left **Wearing Inuit furs to protect him from the harsh Arctic climate, Robert Peary posed for this photograph shortly after his return from the North Pole in April 1909.**

LEAVE OF ABSENCE

Robert Peary joined the U.S. Navy in his mid-twenties and served for his entire working life. The navy not only provided him with a regular income, it also allowed him to pursue his polar ambitions, even though his expeditions often took him away on extended leave. Indeed, Peary was away from his family so often that his daughter complained that her friends thought she was an orphan. Even the loss of nine toes to frostbite, which caused him to walk with a strange sliding step, did not deter Peary from continuing to explore.

GREENLAND

Peary had an aptitude for attracting wealthy backers. Some of America's richest men and most prestigious geographical organizations donated money to support his attempts to reach the North Pole and claim it for the United States. In 1886 and 1891 Peary's groundbreaking expeditions into the desolate interior of Greenland proved that this huge frozen territory was an island. From Greenland, and from the far northern Canadian islands, Peary made several expeditions toward the North Pole.

Peary also studied Greenland's inhabitants, the Inuit, from whom he learned much, particularly how to survive in the freezing Arctic climate. Like the Inuit, Peary often slept outside wrapped in furs, ate his food cold to save on cooking fuel, and, when the temperature plunged, built an igloo for shelter. Peary found much to admire about the Inuit, such as their good nature, their physical strength, and their disinclination to drink alcohol and gamble.

THE NORTH POLE

On February 28, 1909, at the age of fifty-two, Peary set off from Cape Sheridan on Ellesmere Island on his seventh expedition to the Arctic. Intending to reach the North Pole, he took 24 men, 19 sleds, and 133 dogs. Peary's plan was to start out with a large sled party carrying supplies that would be dumped en route and picked up on the return journey. After they put down their loads, sleds returned south. Thus, the party

Above **Peary learned much about survival in the Arctic from native peoples, such as these Inuit from Kosina, Alaska, photographed in 1902.**

MAY 6, 1856
Robert E. Peary is born in Pennsylvania.

1886
Makes first expedition to the Greenland interior.

1891
Proves Greenland is an island.

1898–1902
Explores routes to the North Pole from both Greenland and northern Canada.

1905 AND 1908
Further attempts to reach the Pole fail.

1909
Sled party consisting of Peary, Matthew Henson, four Inuit, and forty dogs claims to have reached the North Pole.

1911
Peary retires from the U.S. Navy.

FEBRUARY 20, 1920
Dies in Washington, DC.

Frederick Albert Cook *1865–1940*

*P*eary's rival was an amiable fraud whose life collapsed around him when his various deceptions were uncovered. Cook lived and worked in Brooklyn and trained as a doctor. From 1891 to 1892, he acted as surgeon on Peary's Greenland expedition. He was also part of the crew of the *Belgica,* which became trapped in the ice for an entire polar winter (1897–1898) while on an international expedition to Antarctica. During that winter, Cook distinguished himself as a cheerful and courageous member of the crew. Roald Amundsen, also on the voyage, described Cook as indispensable.

Cook's desire for fame eventually got the better of him. He caused a sensation with his claim to have reached the North Pole on April 21, 1908, with a small party of Inuit. This claim was soon discredited when Cook failed to produce records to back it up. To Cook's embarrassment, an earlier claim—that he had been the first person to climb Mount McKinley in Alaska, America's highest peak—was proved fraudulent at the same time.

With the loss of his credibility, Cook's career as an explorer was finished. Further misfortune befell him in 1923, when he was sent to prison for an allegedly fraudulent real estate deal he had set up. Cook was innocent and eventually received a pardon from the president of the United States. He died in 1940, insisting until the end of his life that he really had been to the North Pole.

shrank as it traveled north until only a handful of men were left to reach the Pole.

From the outset the journey was easier than it might have been. Especially cold weather had left the ice hard—perfect for sleds and dogs. On April 6, at 1:00 PM, Peary declared that he had reached the North Pole. With him were his loyal assistant Matthew Henson, four Inuit, and forty dogs.

Peary's party returned via the food depots left behind by his sleds. The outward journey had taken forty days; the return trip took just sixteen. Peary had fulfilled a lifetime's ambition and was in no doubt of the magnitude of his achievement.

RIVAL

Barely four days earlier, another American explorer, Frederick Cook, had announced that

Right In 1909 the Parisian *Petit Journal* published this cartoon mocking the battle between Peary and Cook to be recognized as first to plant the U.S. flag at the North Pole. The cartoonist was evidently no wildlife expert: penguins are found in the Antarctic but not in the Arctic.

Le Petit Journal

ADMINISTRATION
61, RUE LAFAYETTE, 61
Les manuscrits ne sont pas rendus

5 CENT. SUPPLÉMENT ILLUSTRÉ 5 CENT.

20ᵐᵉ Année — Numéro 983
DIMANCHE 19 SEPTEMBRE 1909

On s'abonne sans frais dans tous les bureaux de poste

ABONNEMENTS
SEINE et SEINE-ET-OISE... 2 fr. 3 fr. 50
DÉPARTEMENTS............... 2 fr. 4 fr. »
ÉTRANGER.................... 2 50 5 fr. »

POLE NORD

LA CONQUÊTE DU POLE NORD
Le docteur Cook et le commandant Peary s'en disputent la gloire

Peary celebrates his greatest achievement:

The discovery of the North Pole stands for the inevitable victory of courage, persistence, endurance, over all obstacles. . . . The discovery of [this] . . . splendid, frozen jewel of the North, for which through centuries men of every nation have struggled, and suffered and died, is won at last, and is won forever, by the Stars and Stripes!

Robert E. Peary, *The North Pole*

he, too, had reached the Pole. Cook claimed to have achieved his feat a year before Peary. Cook's claim was disputed and soon discredited. Nevertheless, the controversy took the joy from Peary's own triumph. Until his death in 1920, Peary never really shook off the doubts that surrounded his own success.

STOPPING SHORT

During the 1980s researchers examined Peary's expedition log and came to the conclusion that he did not actually reach the North Pole. Owing to poor navigation, it appears that Peary stopped short of the pole—perhaps by as many as thirty miles (50 km), or as few as five miles (8 km). Still, many people agree that this discovery should not detract from his triumph, that the expedition was going so well that the extra few miles were a technicality and may be overlooked. What is indisputable is that Peary and his companions traveled farther north than any explorers before them had done.

SEE ALSO

• Amundsen, Roald
• Exploration and Geographical Societies
• Polar Exploration

PHOTOGRAPHY

SOME OF THE MOST REMARKABLE FEATS OF EXPLORATION of the twentieth century—the ascent of Everest and the first moon landing are two examples—were photographed. These photographs allowed a great number of people to share in the visual impact of the event. Moreover, the photographs survive as permanent visual records that immortalize the explorers and their achievements. Photography of the mid-nineteenth century relied on cumbersome equipment and produced images of poor quality; in the twenty-first century the lightweight digital camera has become an essential part of any explorer's kit bag.

Left **This Daguerre camera dates from 1839 and was made in Paris.**

The first photographs were printed on copper plates in the 1820s and 1830s by such French pioneers as Joseph-Nicéfore Niepce and Louis-Jacques-Mandé Daguerre. Early photographs took several minutes to develop and could not be reproduced. In 1839 an English physicist, W. H. Fox Talbot, invented the calotype process, a technique for printing photographs on paper treated with silver chloride. The calotype was the first photographic process that allowed for multiple images to be reproduced from a single negative. In 1851 Frederick Scott Archer, an English photographer, invented the wet collodion process, which was twenty times faster than

previous methods. However, wet collodion photographs had to be developed immediately, while their coating was still damp.

Two advances in the late nineteenth century improved photography dramatically. The dry-plate negative, invented in 1874, allowed a shot to be developed at a later stage. Although the negative was a bulky glass plate, this method produced a high-quality image and remained popular with explorers until the 1920s. In 1883 George Eastman invented the flexible film strip. Although the quality of the images was not as good as those produced by glass-plate negatives, the film was far smaller and lighter.

Mass Appeal

Prior to the invention of photography, an explorer's visual record of the people, places, and wildlife he or she encountered was a sketch or painting. Travel books were illustrated with expensive hand-colored woodblock or metal-plate engraving, laboriously copied from the original work. The invention of photography allowed even the most unartistic explorers to provide accurate visual records of their expeditions, and the development of mass-printing processes in the late nineteenth century allowed such records to be reprinted cheaply.

Picturing the World

Throughout the second half of the nineteenth century, photographers traveled far and wide to capture exotic landscapes and cultures.

Below **The English photographer Francis Frith took this photograph of the Great Pyramid and Sphinx at Giza, near Cairo, Egypt, in 1858.**

1827
Joseph-Nicéfore Niepce invents the first photographic process.

1831
Louis-Jacques-Mandé Daguerre develops a process later known as the daguerreotype.

1839
W. H. Fox Talbot's calotype photograph provides a negative from which several prints may be made.

1851
Frederick Scott Archer develops the wet collodion process.

1874
Dry-plate glass negatives, which can be developed at a later time, are introduced.

1883
George Eastman invents the film strip.

1914–1916
Frank Hurley photographs Ernest Shackleton's remarkable exploits in the Antarctic.

December 24, 1968
The crew of *Apollo* 8 photograph the earth rising behind the moon.

1985
The remote underwater vessel *Jason-Argo* explores and photographs the wreck of HMS *Titanic*.

Frank Hurley *1885–1962*

*E*rnest Shackleton's expedition to the Antarctic on board the *Endurance* (1914–1916) is one of the great survival stories of the twentieth century. The expedition photographer, Frank Hurley, captured the whole trip on glass-plate negatives. Hurley, born in Australia in 1885, ran away from home at the age of thirteen and, after a short spell working in an iron foundry and then a telegraph office, became a photographer. Hurley had an eye for a dramatic landscape, a talent that enabled him to set up a successful postcard business.

Hurley's shots and movie footage of the *Endurance* trapped in ice and of Shackleton and his team's heroic two-year voyage back to civilization thrilled the world. At one point Hurley dived into icy water in the flooded hold of the sinking *Endurance* in order to retrieve photographs. Both Hurley and Shackleton knew that interest in their expedition would be considerably keener if they provided visual evidence to back up their startling personal accounts.

Their work sparked huge public interest and led to a boom in sales of books and postcards. In western Europe photographers such as Francis Bedford and Francis Frith reproduced staged biblical scenes set in the Holy Land. Their photographs were extremely popular, as they gave Christians an opportunity to see images of places such as Egypt and Palestine, which they had only read of.

Other popular photographic subjects during the nineteenth century included India and China, as well as the recently settled western territories of the United States. From the Utah deserts to the Rocky Mountains, photographers such as William H. Jackson and Eadweard Muybridge found a great deal of lucrative material. The little-known north of Australia and the vast unexplored regions of the Arctic and Antarctic were also prime terri-tory, and Frank Hurley and others forged an international reputation capturing these virgin landscapes.

GREATEST MOMENTS
By the time photography became a standard explorer's tool, most of the world had been discovered, although the world map still contained blank areas. The successes and failures of the pioneering polar explorers Robert Peary, Roald Amundsen, Robert Scott, and Ernest Shackleton were captured in photographs that helped immortalize the men and their achievements. The conquest of Everest by Edmund Hillary in 1953 was also recorded with photographs.

Above **Frank Hurley wearing his polar exploration clothing. After he returned from the Antarctic in 1916, Hurley went straight to France, where he recorded unforgettable images of World War I (1914–1918).**

OUT OF THIS WORLD

The exploration of space produced unforgettable photographs that soon became familiar worldwide. Notable examples include the earth rising over the moon, taken by the crew of *Apollo 8* in 1968, and the first moon walk by Neil Armstrong and Buzz Aldrin in 1969.

Since the nineteenth century, astronomers have made considerable use of photographs of space taken with telescopes. The develop-

Argo-Jason

During the 1970s Robert Ballard, an American marine geologist, developed a series of unmanned deepwater exploration vessels, most notably the *Argo-Jason*. This half-million-dollar platform is equipped with lights, sonar, and still and movie cameras that transmit live images from depths of up to sixteen thousand feet (4,880 m).

Although its cameras have also recorded geological features, the *Argo-Jason* is most famous for exploring in detail the wrecks of HMS *Titanic* and the German battleship *Bismarck*.

ment toward the end of the twentieth century of extremely light-sensitive film and more powerful telescopes revealed the existence of millions of undiscovered galaxies.

OTHER NEW DEVELOPMENTS

At the beginning of the twenty-first century, film began to be superseded by the recording of visual images as digital data. While purists argue that digital technology has yet to match the quality of chemical film, the advantages are obvious. Large numbers of digital photographs may easily be stored, accessed, and transmitted. Whereas film, once developed, can never be reused, a single disk or microchip may be reused any number of times. In addition, an explorer in an isolated location can transmit digital photographs via a satellite phone to the other side of the world almost instantaneously.

Left **This photograph of Buzz Aldrin during the first lunar landing, in 1969, was taken by Neil Armstrong—who can be seen reflected in Aldrin's visor.**

SEE ALSO

- Astronomy • Bishop, Isabella Lucy
- Cousteau, Jacques-Yves • Earth
- Hillary, Edmund • Polar Exploration
- Record Keeping • Shackleton, Ernest Henry
- Underwater Exploration

PIKE, ZEBULON MONTGOMERY

BORN IN NEW JERSEY IN 1779, Zebulon Pike entered the army as a young man. His main exploratory expedition—part geographical survey and part spy mission—produced the first reliable information on the American Southwest. He died in battle during the War of 1812.

ENLISTMENT AND EARLY CAREER

Zebulon Pike's father fought in the American Revolution and remained in the army after the war ended. Young Zebulon received some schooling but preferred the army. At fifteen he enlisted and was assigned to his father's unit. He was stationed on the northern frontier, in the Great Lakes region.

By the age of twenty, Pike had risen to the rank of lieutenant. Over the next few years, he was posted to several different frontier forts in the Great Lakes area. He married and taught himself military tactics, the Spanish and French languages, and some mathematics and science. In 1805 General James Wilkinson, the American governor of the northern part of the Louisiana Territory, sent Pike on his first exploring expedition.

FIRST EXPEDITION

Wilkinson wanted Pike to map the upper Mississippi River, select sites for military and commercial settlements, and invite Native American leaders to Saint Louis. Starting out in early August 1805, Pike led twenty soldiers up the river from Saint Louis. They reached present-day Minnesota as the weather turned cold. Conditions were tough, and the frozen rivers and heavy snowfalls considerably slowed Pike's progress. Leaving some of his men at a small fort they built near present-day Little Falls, Pike, exceeding his orders,

headed north with the rest of his party to try to find the source of the Mississippi. Following one branch of the river, he reached a lake that he identified—incorrectly—as the river's source. The party turned home and reached Saint Louis at the end of April 1806.

Above **Pike unwittingly aided an American conspiracy to seize Spanish land in the Southwest.**

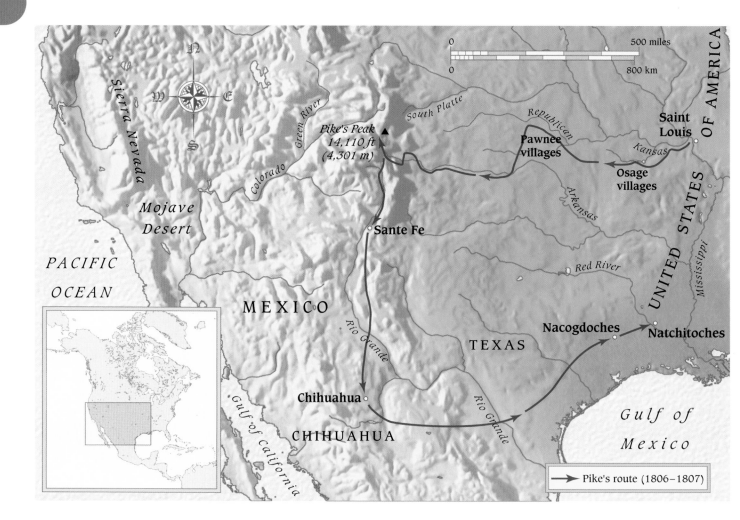

Above **In his journal Pike described the American Southwest as a desert in which white people would never thrive.**

Despite the fact that few Native American chiefs agreed to travel to Saint Louis, Pike signed a treaty with some Sioux chiefs that gave the United States control of the area around present-day Saint Paul and Minneapolis. Later, an army fort was built on the site. He also came across several British trading posts in the area, even though the area belonged to the United States. Pike told the British to leave and warned officials in Washington that the British were promoting hostile feelings among the Native Americans toward U.S. citizens.

A NEW MISSION

Wilkinson soon sent Pike on another journey, this time to the Southwest. First, he was to return some members of the Osage people to their homes in western Missouri and establish friendly relations with other central Great Plains Indians. Second, he was to follow the Arkansas River upstream. Third, he was to find the source of the Red River. Wilkinson also gave Pike secret orders to scout out the strength of Spanish control over the Southwest. Pike set forth with twenty-three men on July 15, 1806.

TO THE SOUTHWEST AND BACK

As he moved through central Missouri, Pike met with the Osage people and later the Pawnees. He had marched halfway across modern Kansas when he learned that Spanish troops—informed of his mission—were looking for him. (Wilkinson, who was secretly collaborating with the Spanish, had actually told the Spanish of Pike's movements, but historians are unsure what prompted him to do so.) Pike and his men turned southwest. Near the Great Bend of the Arkansas River,

Above **A chief of the Osage Indians posed for this portrait in the early 1800s.**

James Wilkinson 1757–1825

James Wilkinson, born in Maryland in 1757, served in the American army during the Revolutionary War. He later settled in Kentucky, where he began many years of intrigues. He worked with Spanish officials to attach Kentucky to the Spanish territory of Louisiana. At the same time he worked to bring Kentucky into the United States. When the Americans bought Louisiana in 1803, Wilkinson—by then commanding general of the U.S. Army—was named governor of the northern part of the area. He began working with Vice President Aaron Burr in a plot to seize Mexico, which Burr would then rule. Wilkinson turned against Burr and revealed the plot. He, like Burr, was tried for his role and found not guilty. When the War of 1812 broke out, he botched an advance against Montreal. He retired from the army in 1815 and died in Texas ten years later.

Pike divided his party and sent some men back to Saint Louis, under the command of Wilkinson's son, with a report on the expedition's findings to that point.

He and the rest of the party followed the Arkansas upstream. By late November they could see the mountain in eastern Colorado that came to be called Pike's Peak. As they had no cold-weather clothing, they could not climb the peak. Pike turned south, and planning to outlast the winter, he and his men built a shelter in southern Colorado. On February 26, 1807, they were captured by Spanish soldiers—an event that probably saved the lives of the exploring party members. Pike claimed that he had believed he was on the Red River when, in fact, he was illegally on the Rio Grande in Spanish territory.

Above **Visible through a narrow pass known as the Gateway is the mountain now called Pike's Peak.**

The Spanish brought Pike and his men through Santa Fe to Chihuahua. On the trip Pike learned much about Mexico. His maps and reports were seized, but he and his men were allowed to return to Louisiana via Texas (a route that showed them more Spanish territory). They arrived home in June 1807.

Pike explains why, having climbed the nine-thousand-foot (2,743 m) Cheyenne Peak, he did not attempt the next mountain farther along (which now bears his name):

The summit of the Grand Peak, which was entirely bare of vegetation and covered with snow, now appeared at the distance of fifteen or sixteen miles from us, and as high again as what we had ascended, and would have taken a whole day's march to have arrived at its base, when I believed no human being could have ascended to its [pinnacle]. . . . [In addition] my soldiers . . . had only light overalls on, and no stockings, and [were in] every way ill provided.

Zebulon M. Pike,
An Account of Expeditions to the Sources of the Mississippi

LATER CAREER

After his return Pike wrote a report of his experiences and drew up maps of the territories he had passed through, basing his work in part on route notes that he had smuggled out of Mexico in the barrels of his men's guns. He suggested that the Southwest was too dry to be useful for farming. He also said that the Spanish hold on the area was weak and that Santa Fe offered the possibility of lucrative trade.

Pike received several promotions, including one to brigadier general after the British and Americans began fighting the War of 1812. In 1813 he died during an American attack on York, Canada (the present-day city of Toronto).

SEE ALSO
- Lewis and Clark Expedition
- Native Peoples
- Spain

PINZÓN, MARTÍN ALONSO

MARTÍN ALONSO PINZÓN (c. 1441–1493) was a key participant in Christopher Columbus's historic 1492 voyage west across the Atlantic. Martín Pinzón helped Columbus secure the approval of the king and queen of Spain, invested in the venture himself, and commanded one of the expedition's ships. Despite his valuable contribution as a navigator, Martín Pinzón deserted Columbus—probably on two occasions—and is remembered primarily for his disloyalty.

PIONEER

Martín Pinzón was born into a family of navigators and shipowners in the southern Spanish town of Palos. Martín, who became a sailor in accordance with family tradition, took an early interest in Columbus's plan to reach Asia by traveling west.

Although historical records are inconclusive, it is possible that, in 1488, the French port of Dieppe employed Pinzón to accompany Jean Cousin on a voyage along the west coast of Africa. A severe storm is alleged to have blown Cousin hundreds of miles to the west, where he reached a strange land and a huge river. If the story is true, then Cousin, with Martín Pinzón on board, reached the Americas (probably Brazil) four years before Columbus.

This adventure would certainly explain Pinzón's willingness to support the Columbus expedition. Another possible explanation for Pinzón's enthusiasm is his visit, during the late 1480s, to Rome, where he learned of voyages by Norse navigators to Vinland (present-day Newfoundland) in the eleventh century.

1441	1488	1492	1493	
Martín Alonso Pinzón is born in Palos, Spain.	Possibly accompanies Jean Cousin on an expedition along the coast of West Africa, during which their ship is blown off course and perhaps reaches Brazil.	Supports Columbus's crossing of the Atlantic. Captains the *Pinta* but deserts Columbus in the Caribbean.	Rejoins Columbus but deserts him again in the Azores; dies.	*Above* **Martín Alonso Pinzón was one of three brothers who sailed with Columbus to the Americas.**

Above **These illustrations of Columbus's discovery of the island of Hispaniola were engraved in 1493 and accompanied the printed version of a letter Columbus wrote to one of his sponsors.**

COLUMBUS'S SUPPORTER

Martín Pinzón contributed greatly to Columbus's preparation for his 1492 expedition by persuading royal advisers that the voyage was worth backing. Pinzón himself put up a one-eighth share of the expenses. He also helped find two of the ships, the *Pinta* and the *Niña,* and recruited crew members.

Once the voyage had begun, Martín Pinzón captained the *Pinta,* on which his brother Francisco was the pilot. His other brother, Vicente Yáñez Pinzón, captained the *Niña.* It was at Martín's suggestion that Columbus changed course on October 7, a decision that led to land being sighted five days later.

DESERTION

On November 21, 1492, Martín Pinzón deserted Columbus, probably to search for gold, and became the first European to set foot on the island that Columbus later named Hispaniola. On January 6 he rejoined the main expedition and, under suspicion of treason, set off on the return journey to Spain.

At the Azores, Columbus (aboard the *Niña*) and Pinzón (aboard the *Pinta*) were parted once more. The ships may have been separated by storms, although it is more likely that Pinzón attempted to upstage Columbus by arriving in Spain before him. Pinzón reached Spain first, but the king and queen ordered him to wait for Columbus. Disgraced, disheartened, and sick, Martín Pinzón died a few weeks later.

Vinland

According to one Icelandic saga written during the thirteenth century, the Norse sailor Leif Eriksson was blown off course while heading for Greenland around 1000 CE. Eriksson landed in North America and the following year found an area he named Vinland ("wine land") after the grapes that grew there. It is possible that stories of Vinland inspired Pinzón to participate in Columbus's expedition.

SEE ALSO

- Columbus, Christopher
- Pinzón, Vicente Yáñez

PINZÓN, VICENTE YÁÑEZ

BORN INTO A CELEBRATED SPANISH SEAFARING FAMILY, Vicente Yáñez Pinzón (1460–c. 1523) captained the *Niña* on Columbus's historic 1492 voyage. In 1499, perhaps acting on information provided by his elder brother, Martín Alonso Pinzón, Vicente led his own voyage to the Americas, on which he reached the mouth of the Amazon River in Brazil. Vicente Pinzón made at least three further voyages to the Americas. On one he and his fellow explorer Juan Díaz de Solís (c. 1470–1516) sailed along the coast of Mexico.

LOYAL LIEUTENANT

Vicente Pinzón was one of three brothers who sailed with Columbus across the Atlantic to the Caribbean in 1492. He was captain of the *Niña* and, unlike his elder brother Martín, Vicente remained loyal to Columbus through the entirety of the voyage. Indeed, it was on the *Niña* that Columbus chose to set up his command when his flagship, the *Santa María*, ran aground.

It is possible that, before his death in 1493, Martín Pinzón told Vicente of a voyage he had made in 1488 to a land divided by a huge river that lay somewhere to the south of the islands discovered by Columbus. In 1499 Vicente led his own expedition across the Atlantic Ocean. He sailed from Palos, Spain, with four ships and, steering farther to the south than Columbus had done, reached present-day Recife on the coast of Brazil on January 20, 1500.

Left **This portrait of Vicente Yáñez Pinzón was painted by Julio Garcia Condoy.**

c. 1460	1500	1506	c. 1523
Vicente Yáñez Pinzón is born in Palos, Spain.	Discovers the Amazon River.	Explores Yucatán Peninsula with Juan Díaz de Solís.	Dies.
1492–1493	**1505**		
Captains the *Niña* on Columbus's historic transatlantic voyage.	Is appointed governor of Puerto Rico.	**1508–1509** Searches for a sea passage west to the Spice Islands.	

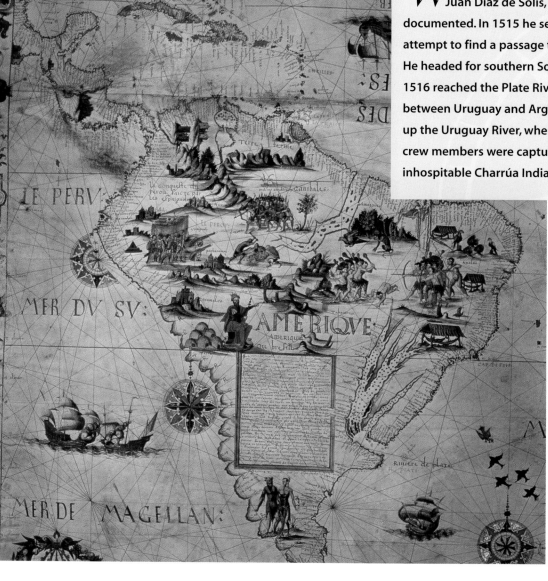

Left Although this 1550 French map of South America clearly shows the Amazon and Plate Rivers and records the coast in some detail, much of the interior is a product of the cartographer's imagination.

The Amazon and Mexico

Vicente Pinzón spent four months exploring the coast of Brazil. Historical records name him as the official discoverer of the Amazon River—which he at first believed to be the Ganges River, some eight thousand miles (13,000 km) away, in India.

After additional voyages to the New World, in 1505 Vicente Pinzón was rewarded by the Spanish crown with the governorship of Puerto Rico, an island in the Caribbean. The following year he explored the western Caribbean with Juan Díaz de Solís. Precisely where Pinzón and Díaz de Solís went is not known, but they were probably the first Europeans to set eyes on the coast of Mexico.

On his final voyage (also in the company of Díaz de Solís), Pinzón's task was to find a passage westward to the Spice Islands (the present-day Moluccas in Southeast Asia). He and Díaz de Solís explored southward along the coast of South America as far as the Río Negro in central Argentina. However, the two men did not get on well with each other, and their expedition was cut short. They returned to Spain in August 1509.

SEE ALSO

- Columbus, Christopher
- Pinzón, Martín Alonso

Polar Exploration

THE NORTH AND SOUTH POLES are the northern and southern ends, respectively, of the axis around which the earth spins. The name for the region around the North Pole, the Arctic, derives from the Greek word *arctos,* which refers to the constellation that appears in the northern sky (a constellation known in English as the Great Bear). The southern polar region is called Antarctica, which means "opposite the Arctic." With freezing temperatures and months of total darkness, the Arctic and Antarctic are the most hostile places on earth and, unsurprisingly, were among the last of the earth's regions to be reached by explorers.

EARLY POLAR VOYAGES

Polar exploration began in the sixteenth and seventeenth centuries with English and Dutch voyages to the north. The aim of the first polar explorers was to find a shortcut to Asia. At the time it was not known that most of the Arctic was a vast frozen sea. Those early explorers, hoping to find open navigable waters, discovered fields of ice, where their ships were battered by blizzards and were in constant danger of being frozen in or crushed.

Finding the way due north blocked, the explorers searched for a northeast or a northwest passage to Asia. Conditions were as bad in both directions. In 1553 Sir Hugh Willoughby, who had been searching northeast, froze to death with all his men on the coast of Lapland (northern Scandinavia). In 1611 Henry Hudson, who had sailed northwest, was cast adrift in a small boat by his mutinous crew in Hudson Bay, never to be seen again. It took great courage—or foolhardiness—to lead an expedition into the Arctic.

Right **This photograph, from Robert F. Scott's 1911 expedition, shows the frozen sea at the base of the Beardmore Glacier, the edge of the Antarctic continent. To reach the South Pole, Scott had to climb this glacier.**

QUEST FOR THE NORTH POLE

Early polar expeditions were launched with practical aims, such as the search for new trade routes. From the nineteenth century onward, polar expeditions were launched with the sole aim of exploring uncharted regions of the earth. Many explorers were motivated by a patriotic desire to win honor for their country. Others were motivated to test themselves to the limit.

In 1827 an English naval officer, William Parry, made the first attempt to reach the North Pole. He sailed to the Arctic island of Spitsbergen, to the north of Scandinavia, planning to continue over the ice on sleds and small boats. Parry hoped to find a flat ice sheet that he could sled over. Instead, he discovered that the ice was broken up by many narrow stretches of open water. His men made very slow progress as, again and again, they repeated the cycle of dragging their boats over the ice and launching them into the water. On July 20, Parry calculated that, although he had traveled twelve miles (19 km) in the previous three days, he was only five miles (8 km) farther north. The southward drift of the Arctic ice sheet was carrying Parry backward almost as fast as he could move forward.

Right **While Fridtjof Nansen's *Fram* was frozen in the ice, the expedition botanist, Henrik Blessing, made scientific observations. Here he is collecting algae with a long pole.**

1596
Willem Barents discovers Spitsbergen.

1607
Henry Hudson reaches a point 577 miles (929 km) from the North Pole.

1772–1775
James Cook sails around Antarctica.

JANUARY 27, 1820
Fabian Gottlieb von Bellingshausen sights the Antarctic continent.

1827
William Parry makes his first attempt to reach the North Pole.

1839–1843
James Clark Ross discovers and names Ross Ice Shelf and Victoria Land in the Antarctic.

1893–1896
Fridtjof Nansen attempts to drift to the North Pole in the *Fram*.

1901–1904
Robert F. Scott spends three winters in Antarctica and, with Ernest Shackleton, makes the first attempt to reach the South Pole.

1908
Ernest Shackleton gets to within 112 miles (180 km) of the South Pole.

1909
Robert E. Peary claims to have reached the North Pole.

Arctic Drift

*T*he Arctic (like the other seas) has powerful currents, which cause the ice sheets to drift at a considerable rate. William Parry made the unfortunate discovery of Arctic currents in 1827, and their existence was proved in 1881, when wreckage from a ship that had been crushed in the ice above Siberia was found to have drifted across the Arctic to Greenland.

In 1893 the Norwegian explorer Fridtjof Nansen (1861–1930) attempted to take advantage of the Arctic currents to reach the North Pole. He deliberately allowed a specially strengthened ship, the *Fram*, to become frozen into the ice north of Russia and then waited for the currents to carry him to his goal.

After two years had passed, it was clear that the *Fram* was going to drift south of the Pole rather than over it. So, on March 14, 1895, Nansen abandoned his ship and set off over the ice with one companion. For almost a month, Nansen struggled north on dogsleds before he realized, as William Parry had done in 1827, that the drift was carrying him backward almost as fast as he could go forward. On April 8, 226 miles (363 km) from the North Pole, Nansen turned back.

1911
Roald Amundsen is the first person to reach the South Pole.

1912
Having reached the South Pole, Robert F. Scott dies on the return trip.

1914–1916
Ernest Shackleton makes his third Antarctic expedition.

1926
U.S. pilot Richard Byrd flies to the North Pole.

1929
Byrd flies over the South Pole.

1955–1956
Twelve nations set up Antarctic scientific bases.

1986
The U.S. explorer Ann Bancroft becomes the first woman to reach the North Pole overland.

1990
Erling Kagge makes the first unsupported expedition to the North Pole.

1993
Bancroft leads an all-female expedition to the South Pole.

1993
Erling Kagge makes the first solo unsupported expedition to the South Pole.

Above **James Clark Ross, the most experienced polar explorer of his time.**

In 1595 Gerrit de Veer, who sailed in search of a northeast passage with the Dutch explorer Willem Barents, described one particular peril of the Arctic:

Two of our men lying together in one place, a great lean white bear came stealing out, and caught one of them fast by the neck who, not perceiving what it was, cried out and said, "Who is it that pulls me so by the neck?" . . . The bear . . . falling upon the man, bit his head asunder and sucked out the blood, wherewith the rest of the men that were on the land, ran presently thither. . . . She, perceiving them to come towards her, fiercely ran at them, and getting another of them . . . tore him in pieces.

Quoted in the *Oxford Book of Exploration*

ANTARCTICA

Unlike the Arctic, which is mostly sea, Antarctica includes a vast ice-covered continental landmass—the highest, coldest, and windiest continent on earth. For centuries people theorized that there might be a great continent in the Southern Hemisphere to balance those of the north. Many maps of the sixteenth and seventeenth centuries included a huge mythical landmass, generally labeled *Terra Australis* (southern land).

During the second half of the eighteenth century, as a series of voyages penetrated farther south into sub-Antarctic latitudes, the area that might be covered by such a continent was greatly reduced. In 1772 the English Royal Navy sent Captain James Cook to look for a southern continent. On a voyage that lasted three years, Cook sailed all the way around Antarctica without realizing that he had done so. Although he did not see the continent, he was sure that it was there, for he saw a great many icebergs—which originate on land.

The first recorded sightings of Antarctica were made in 1820 on three separate expeditions, sent by Britain, the United States, and Russia. The explorer usually given the credit for the discovery of Antarctica is Fabian Gottlieb von Bellingshausen, who recorded seeing the Fimbul Ice Shelf on January 27, 1820, from on board the Russian ship *Vostock*. Bellingshausen had been guided in part by reports from a nineteen-year-old sealer from Connecticut named Nathaniel D. Palmer.

During the 1840s American and English explorers mapped extensive parts of the Antarctic coastline. In 1840 Charles Wilkes, an American naval captain, charted nearly 1,500 miles (2,414 km) of the region now identified as Wilkes Land. On a separate voyage around the same time, the English explorer James Clark Ross mapped a large part of the coast of Antarctica (1839–1843), which he named

Victoria Land after the English queen. Among Ross's more remarkable discoveries was a live volcano, belching smoke, which he named Mount Erebus after one of his ships. He discovered an ice sheet, joined to the continent, that was later named the Ross Ice Shelf in his honor.

TO THE SOUTH POLE

Between 1897 and 1917, a total of nine countries sent sixteen expeditions to Antarctica. In 1902 the British explorer Robert Falcon Scott made the first attempt to reach the South Pole, using sleds pulled by dogs. Scott was forced to abandon his journey when one of his team, Ernest Shackleton, fell ill with scurvy.

In 1908 Shackleton himself returned to Antarctica as leader of his own expedition. He climbed the Beardmore Glacier onto the South Polar Plateau, a wide, flat area 7,200 feet (2,200 km) above sea level. Although he got to within 112 miles (180 km) of the South Pole, he turned back, having decided that the risk was too great for his men, who were weakened by the cold and by the shortage of food.

Above **This eighteenth-century French engraving depicts Inuit hunters struggling to overcome polar bears.**

AMUNDSEN AND SCOTT

In 1911 the quest for the South Pole became a race between the Norwegian Roald Amundsen and the Englishman Robert Falcon Scott. On December 12, 1911, the race was won by Amundsen and his team. On January 17, 1912, Scott arrived at the pole to find the Norwegian flag planted in the ice. Scott and his party of five all died of cold, starvation, and scurvy on their return journey.

MODERN EXPEDITIONS

In 1990 Erling Kagge, a Norwegian, became the first explorer to reach the North Pole with no assistance from dogs or motorized equipment. Three years later he walked alone to the South Pole. In 1986 and 1993 an American, Ann Bancroft, became the first woman to reach the poles.

Right **The photographer Herbert Ponting took moving footage and many still photographs during Scott's 1911 Antarctic expedition.**

Reaching the South Pole

Amundsen and Scott reached the South Pole within five weeks of each other, although their methods were very different. Amundsen equipped his men with fur clothing and brought tough Inuit dogs from northern Greenland. Scott's men, on the other hand, wore layers of canvas and woolen clothing, twice the weight of Amundsen's and neither as warm nor as waterproof. Scott's men traveled with ponies and motor sleds, which were unsuited to the Antarctic terrain. Scott's plan was to use manpower to haul his sled for the last part of the journey. He wrote, "when a party of men go forth to face hardships, dangers and difficulties with their own unaided efforts . . . the conquest is more nobly and splendidly won."

SEE ALSO

- Amundsen, Roald • Baffin, William
- Bellingshausen, Fabian Gottlieb von
- Bering, Vitus Jonassen • Byrd, Richard E.
- Clothing • Cook, James

- Hudson, Henry • Illness and Disease
- Land Transport • Nansen, Fridtjof
- Nordenskiöld, Nils Adolf Erik
- Northeast Passage

- Northwest Passage • Peary, Robert E
- Scott, Robert Falcon
- Shackleton, Ernest Henry
- Southern Continent

GLOSSARY

Aztec A member of a people who ruled a large empire in central and southern Mexico during the fifteenth century, before the arrival of the Spanish conquistadores.

botany The branch of biology dealing with plants.

chronometer A clock capable of keeping accurate time on board a ship. The name derives from two Greek words: *chronos* (time) and *metron* (measure).

creditor One who lends money or to whom money is owed.

ford A place where a river is shallow enough to be crossed.

hidalgo A member of the lower Spanish nobility.

iceberg A floating mountain of ice; an iceberg is formed when a slab of ice breaks off a glacier (a frozen river) as it reaches the sea.

Inuit A member of a people living in Greenland and northern Canada, inside the Arctic circle. The word *inuit* is the plural of *inuk,* which means "person" in the Inuit language.

isthmus A narrow bridge of land connecting two larger land areas.

Louisiana Territory The land west of the Mississippi River, encompassing the drainage basins of the Missouri and Arkansas Rivers, purchased by President Thomas Jefferson from France in 1803.

magnet stone A naturally magnetic iron ore, also called magnetite.

malaria A fever caused by a parasite transmitted by the bite of the female anopheles mosquito.

negative An image captured on chemically treated film or on a glass plate, with light and dark areas reversed, from which multiple positive photographic images may be produced.

Osage A member of a Native American people that lived on the central Great Plains.

Pawnee A member of a Great Plains Indian people that lived in earth lodges along the Platte River, raised crops, and hunted buffalo.

pioneer The first person to attain a given goal, such as a feat of exploration, the settlement of a new territory, or the invention of a new technology.

Sioux A member of a Native American people that lived on the northern Great Plains and as far east as southern Minnesota.

sled A vehicle with runners instead of wheels; a sled is used to transport people and goods over snow-covered terrain or over the ice.

sonar A system, similar in conception to radar, that uses sound waves to detect objects underwater.

taxonomy Classification of plants and animals according to the natural relationship between them; also the study of different methods of classification.

trading post In North America, a settlement where European traders and Native American hunters exchanged goods for furs.

treason The crime of acting to overthrow or kill the monarch or government of the state to which the criminal owes allegiance.

Viking A term, from a Norwegian word meaning both "pirate" and "warfare," used generally to refer to a Scandinavian (someone from Norway, Sweden, or Denmark) during the years 790 to 1100; especially, any of the Norse raiders who plundered the coasts of western Europe in that period.

INDEX